The Strength of Government

The Godkin Lectures at Harvard University, 1968

The Godkin Lectures on the Essentials of

Free Government and the Duties of the Citizen

were established at Harvard University in 1903

in memory of Edwin Lawrence Godkin (1831–1902).

They are given annually under the auspices of the

John Fitzgerald Kennedy School of Government.

The Strength of Government

by McGeorge Bundy

Cambridge, Massachusetts, 1968

Harvard University Press

The Author

McGeorge Bundy is president of the Ford Foundation. From 1961 to 1966 he served Presidents Kennedy and Johnson as Special Assistant for National Security Affairs. Before that he served Harvard University as professor of government and Dean of the Faculty of Arts and Sciences.

Contents

Introduction

This little book is written in praise of strong government and active participation therein. It is the written version of a set of Godkin lectures delivered at Harvard in March 1968. I have tidied them up a little for publication, and in a few places I have expanded the argument to take account of helpful comments from friends. But I have made no effort to change their somewhat informal and personal tone, and that tone deserves a word of explanation.

These lectures were framed as suggestions from a participant in public affairs to a university audience. I have been in academic life, but never primarily a scholar, and it was clear to me that what I might have to say to my old colleagues and to the present university population could not be based on any claim to a scholar's mastery, but only on the possible value of a participant's observations. Not the least of the advantages of this choice was that it simplified my task. The rules of discourse for the actor are not the same as for the scholar. The actor may be more declarative and less analytic; he may make his point more by illustration than by exhausting the evidence. Moreover a public man may do what a scholar may not—he may plunder the work of others for his purposes with never a footnote of acknowledgment, counting it somehow a sufficient tribute that he takes the scholar's thought for his own. I am indebted to those who have said many of these things earlier and often better, even where I cannot trace their influence directly. About this particular deviation from the rules of scholarship, however, I feel no shame. I think it is much more important, in politics, to get things right than to get them first, and to some degree each of us has to learn such things for himself in any case.

I took advantage in Cambridge of the notion that a public man's opinions can be useful raw material for scholars and students even when they are not approved. On this ground I allowed myself an occasional quite personal and undefended judgment on a particular issue—a course which was made necessary also by the large topic I had chosen and the sharp constraint of the three hours assigned to the lectures. This rather assertive style is less appropriate in a book; so I have removed some of my more sweeping *obiter dicta* and tried to buttress some of the others. Readers who are offended by what is left have my apologies, but there is a limit to the amount of revision such lectures can endure.

* * * *

The personal tone of the argument is related also to the special shape of its original audience. I was aiming at the Harvard community and especially at that part of it which is politically engaged. In revising the lectures I have tried to remove some of the most narrowly parochial elements of that rhetorical posture so as not to limit myself to Harvard men, but I have not changed my general target. Especially in the last chapter I have directly defined that target as "the university audience," and I have addressed myself in particular to those under thirty.

It is far from clear to me that this has proved a successful form of address. I found in Cambridge that there is a considerable distance between men of my experience and the college activist of today. After a week of discussion I was reinforced in my conviction that the distance between the young and the middle-aged can be bridged, but I was not at all certain that in these lectures I had bridged it. In revising them I have tried to take account of what I learned from new friends in Cambridge, but I may not have learned enough.

Yet I do not repent of my temerity in attempting to address the present university audience directly. Their generation and mine are stuck with each other, and if we are to learn the art of peaceful coexistence, we shall have to practice that of communication.

My principal obligations, however, are to people more nearly my own age. I owe special thanks to a small group of good friends and critics who have helped me with candid comment on the present argument: Francis Bator, David Bell, David Ginsburg, Kermit Gordon, Carl Kaysen, Archibald MacLeish, Robert McNamara, Richard Neustadt, Don Price, David Riesman, and Mitchell Sviridoff. None of all this is their fault, but it would have been worse without them. I owe a different but equal debt to my friend Max Hall of Harvard University Press; he is a servant of clarity. Here as elsewhere in the day's work I would be helpless without Alice

Boyce and Elsa Mejia; they know my handwriting and they know the subject. Finally, I must express the indebtedness my wife and I feel to Mr. and Mrs. Henry Redmond. They are kind landlords in an unkind world, and their house is a happy place to work in.

* * * *

Rhetorically, at least, there is a difficulty in presenting an argument for greater strength in our government in a year when many of our most concerned and conscientious citizens are inclined to believe that it is precisely the strength of a government they disagree with that has brought us to great trouble in Vietnam. Vietnam is a separate subject, and I do not presume to suppose that I could hope at this late date to change the views of any of those who have deeply held opinions on the matter—on either side. But I noticed in Cambridge that their passionate opinion on Vietnam had persuaded some good men that all strong government is bad. I respect their feelings, but I think they should reconsider their logic. The argument of this book is entirely independent of Vietnam, and of the use of Presidential power in that contest. I myself would argue that those who would have stayed out of Vietnam, or limited our effort more sharply, should in fact be advocates of stronger and not weaker powers in the Presidency, but I seek no debate right now on that contested question. I content myself with asking those who have strong feelings about Vietnam to consider how much power they would give to a President they approved. If it turns out that they would give him quite a lot, then I will count them on my side of the present argument.

I have sought in this book to avoid any trespass on the rela- tions of confidence which I had as a staff officer in the White House from 1961 to 1966. Such evidence as I present, indeed, is drawn mainly from outside my own direct experience in the government. I think it a sound general rule that staff men should not engage in public reminiscences—if ever—until their principals are well off stage. An exception exists, obviously, when a President would himself want the job done, as we may be sure that President Kennedy would have wanted the brilliant books of Sorensen and Schlesinger. He would see them as the best available substitutes for the book he himself was planning. But President Kennedy had no great opinion of my skills as a writer, and the things I might add are mostly things I think he would not want added now. As for his successor, to whom I am also bound by ties that are more than formal, I reveal no secret when I say that he has not pressed his White House staff to rush into print.

The theme of this book is the need for stronger government in the United States—for government strong enough, at all levels and in all branches, to meet explosive needs that no other force can handle. I believe that for the sake of our own future freedom we must now find ways to make our system of government more effective—not necessarily larger, certainly not more intrusive, and above all not less responsive to our own opinions and desires—but stronger just the same. I have come to these beliefs out of more than twenty years of study and experience, beginning in 1946 when I was working for Henry L. Stimson. I think Mr. Stimson would agree with my argument. I am sure he would agree with my wish to do honor to two other men from whom I learned even more, but

xii   whose approval of the argument I have no right to claim. So I dedicate this volume to the two Presidents for whom I have worked—John F. Kennedy and Lyndon B. Johnson—two strong servants of the cause of effective government.

McGeorge Bundy

New York, May 28, 1968

The Strength of Government

1

Explosive Need

"The essentials of free government and the duties of the citizen." This, or "some aspect thereof," is the assigned topic of the Godkin Lecturer. My own decision is to discuss this topic in the light of what we are learning to call the age of explosions—explosions of technology, of purpose, and of human need which intersect to make ours at once the most dangerous and the most hopeful time in history. What are the essentials of free government in such a time? Always supposing that the true end of government is freedom, do we need more government, or less, or different?

I intend to argue

1. that these explosions require stronger government,
2. that a chief practical obstacle to progress is the present weakness of our governing process, and
3. that this process can be greatly improved if people like you and me do a better job as citizens.

In making my case I intend to take several things for granted. One premise is that we know what we mean when we say that the object of government is freedom. In some rough way, I assume, we are agreed on the content of that work. The Bill of Rights enters into it. The Four Freedoms also say something about it: freedom from want and freedom from fear are essential parts of it. But it also means freedom to be more of a person—freedom to realize that is possible for you, and here as in more negative aspects the tradition of Harvard

4   is connected with it. I find a lot of it in Alfred North White-head and even more in William James, but most of all for our present purpose I will summon as examples of its meaning the names of some of Harvard's public men: of Holmes and Brandeis, of Theodore and Franklin Roosevelt, and of John Kennedy. This is no definition of freedom, only an assumption defended by the good company of others who have shared it.

Another of my premises is that the system of government as it stands today is in fact an instrument that can be made to work for freedom. As against starting over again—by moving outside the existing social and political structure or by trying to knock it down—I believe it is better to try to move on from where we are. In my judgment the American polity, with all its faults, is today the best and strongest there is, at least among major nations. You may look around the world and call that faint praise; so let me add a still stronger statement: that I know of no society in this generation which has a better record of sustained success in the service of human freedom than our own. But I am beginning to offer argument where I intend only to state assumption. I am assuming that the thing to do with our government is to keep it and improve it, not to discard it and start over.

I am also assuming that the citizen can and should have an active part in making his government work—that such "duties of the citizen" are real and important. In Chapter 3 I shall try to buttress this assumption by argument, but I mention it at the outset because it affects the direction of my argument in earlier chapters; my interest in what is wrong derives largely from my belief that we can fix it if we will. Rightly or wrongly, I reject the notion that any American is forced to be merely a passive object of our national political process. I assume that one of "the duties of the citizen" is in fact to take part, and I do not mean merely that he should vote and then feel good about it—as if the election were some pious act of righteous devotion to democracy. I assume instead a right and duty to help in the real business of trying to govern for freedom.

So far I have noted three premises: that we know what freedom is—that the existing governmental structure is the right one to work with—and that we can and should bear a hand. These are substantial premises—and let me end the preliminaries by noting a still larger one: that these premises are yours too. This is obviously presumptuous. I know that a very few undergraduates really do believe in tearing the whole thing down, and that some believe politics and government are good things to stay away from completely. I remember professors too, and unless they have changed there are excellent men among them who just don't care that much about all this. In my fourth premise I intend no discredit or discourtesy to such members of the university community. Nor do I intend to force the pace with others who may have more specific reservations about any of my premises. Indeed I would be disappointed if there were not many who think it too easy to assert that we know what we mean by freedom. It is indeed too easy, and the unending examination of the meaning of that and other great human ends is an indispensable part of the life of a university.

I make my fourth assumption, in short, knowing that in some indeterminate degree it is contrary to fact. I hope it is more true than false, but my first purpose in making it is to

6   lay a base not for the substance of my argument, but for its rhetorical direction. I think I can make myself better understood if I assume that you are making this particular suspension of disbelief. If we assume for now that we can have a part in making this government work for freedom, you will not have to accept my argument, but at least you may be able to understand a little better how it feels to the man who is making it. That would be a real gain, because one of the great necessities of the modern polity is that those who take part in it should develop a stronger capacity to understand the thought and action of one another.

*   *   *   *

My first general proposition is that the age of explosion requires stronger government. I intend the proposition in the sense that we need stronger government for the sake of freedom. I think it highly likely that there is a still deeper necessity—almost an iron law—that will force more government upon us whether or not that government serves freedom. We shall see this stern necessity at the edges of our argument, but my own starting point is more optimistic and purposive: my case for government is that we need it for our own good purposes. To make that case I offer three great areas where explosive change has dramatically increased the requirement for action: the struggle against racism and poverty, the revolution in communication, and the existence of nuclear weapons. All are familiar subjects, but familiarity and understanding are not always the same thing.

I pick these three cases for several reasons. They are stubborn and continuing problems which will still be there at the end of the century. They are very different from one another in their specific shape and size—they all require stronger government, but in deeply different ways, so that they tend to illustrate different aspects of the general problem I have chosen. Finally, I choose them because not one of them will force me directly into a political posture as defender of the acts of the Kennedy and Johnson administrations. I think issues which engage that loyalty should be discussed in some other forum.

*   *   *   *

The more we learn about race and poverty the more we feel the force of two contrasting propositions: the first is that the problem is enormously complex and deep-rooted, and the second is that it can be solved. It is this double awareness, on which the Negro himself has learned to insist, that makes the problem explosive, and there will be only explosions, not solutions, if there is not action by government at every level.

The components of the problem are now usually seen as jobs, housing, welfare, and education. In all four fields the role of government has public recognition. This recognition is plainer in some fields than in others, and many of us have protective devices which allow us to believe ourselves friendly to a good cause and still hostile to government. Thus there are men who manage to combine sentimental support for education with a general hostility to "governmental interference," neglecting the fact that our public school systems, large and small, north and south, are themselves an arm of government—mainly state and local government,

8   it is true, but not for that reason less a part of the world of
politics. School teachers and administrators greatly contribute
to this general error by their own insistence that schools
should be kept "out of politics." They mean that cheap
clubhouse politics should be avoided, but the public mind
registers a quite different impression—namely that the
quality of public life and the quality of the schools are
unrelated. The upshot is that most school systems remain
subject to petty politics and that in most parts of the country
public education lacks the true political champion it needs.
A similarly misleading process of thought operates in welfare,
and with almost as little excuse, for there the role of government at every level has been large for thirty years.

In housing and jobs there is more excuse for confusion. It
is still true, after all, that the lion's share of the building and
employing is done by others than the government. It is reasonable to think of the government as an auxiliary force, and
not as the primary direct agent. But that auxiliary role remains indispensable, and the simplest demonstration is that
the over-all job level, which is probably the most powerful
single variable affecting poverty and race in the country,
most plainly depends upon the fiscal and monetary policy
of government. Nothing in American behavior is more
peculiar than the national reluctance to accept in words
what is taken for granted in fact: that in our general economic
life the government has affirmative responsibilities which
derive quite simply from necessity.

It is high time for all of us to agree that if we take it as a
proper goal of our society to put an end to poverty and racial

oppression—and surely this is not a proposition I need take time to debate—then there is work which only government can do. To the simple, if somehow troublesome, argument that every relevant field of action is already of necessity a field of government action, we can add two special factors which still further identify the government, and in particular the federal government, as the necessary agent of action. These are the financial costs of the job and the necessity of active pressure against prejudice.

No one really knows what it will cost to end poverty and racial unfairness in America. For our present purposes there is no need to know. Clearly this cause can use several times as much money as the Congress can yet be expected to vote for, even on the most optimistic assumptions about domestic politics, public opinion, and Vietnam. My own rough estimate is that the kind of new money we need, above and beyond our important but fragmentary present efforts, is of the order of thirty billions a year. I further believe that as one part of the battle becomes less demanding, opportunity and need will tend to appear elsewhere, so that it is wrong to suppose that these are short-term figures. Some of the necessary money can and should come from other sources, and often the role of government can be more catalytic than controlling, but in one way or another a nationwide effort on this scale will inevitably mean federal action.

To me the element of cost, though decisive in itself, is less interesting than the element of need for the government as the one most effective instrument against prejudice. This is the proposition that General Eisenhower so strongly denied

10   in his repeated—and obviously sincere—assertion that
government cannot change the way men think. I think the
overwhelming evidence is that he has got the argument the
wrong way around. I believe that it is precisely because it is
so hard for anyone to change the minds of men—hard but not
impossible—that we must turn to the instruments of government. Obviously at the limit of the argument General Eisenhower is correct; no one anywhere is going to make everyone
in Mississippi think like Chief Justice Warren overnight.
But when we consider what the government has done to
affect men's thinking in the last twenty-five years, it becomes
absurd to disconnect it from this problem. American soldiers
think differently about the Negro because of a whole series of
government decisions, and landlords near some military bases
are now revising their attitudes for the same reason. Re-
formers rightly remark on the unacceptably slow pace of
change in the schools, but there is change just the same, and
it begins with a decision of the Supreme Court. When we
look beyond the federal government to state and local
authority there is still more evidence at hand. If police are
integrated and if they are humane (which may be just as
important), it is because an agency of government has acted;
a good mayor or good police leadership has shown the way.
Where school systems have done more than the necessary
foot-dragging minimum, it is because of government. And
where Negroes themselves have begun to assume political
authority in mixed communities—where we have moved
from the time of Adam Clayton Powell, the flamboyant tribune
of the neglected, to the time of the promising mayors of all

the people—there the transforming role of government may
be clearest of all.

Yet the role of state and local governments is not always constructive, and indeed the force of such authorities in sustaining discrimination is one of the most compelling arguments for a necessary federal role on the other side. When we seek to attack prejudice, we are not dealing with the minds of men alone, but also with the instruments of action that those minds have put into effect. What lesser governments have done to give free rein to prejudice must be undone before we can overcome racism. And very often the necessary action can come only from Washington. The example of the schools is familiar, but I myself think the matter of equal access to real estate may be still more fundamental: this country cannot have real decency in its race relations until it turns clear away from the notions of right and wrong embodied in the belief that the ownership of a piece of property carries with it the right to decide that no black man shall own it next. We shall have to have open purchase and rental of all real property before we are through. To put it bluntly, the average real estate man must change his position on this point, and there is no reason to suppose that he will do so except as that position becomes a federal offense.*

* This passage, like others dealing with open housing, was written before the passage of the Civil Rights Act of 1968 and the remarkable decision of the Supreme Court in Jones v. Mayer Co. These actions of the federal government take us a long way in the direction I here advocate, but I suspect that still more federal powers will be needed in the end.

12   It is only too easy, in this business of prejudice, to fall into the error of taking pleasure in stating necessities like these. Such statements can serve as an emotional release for the understandable anger that is stirred by the contrast between the righteous language of the Association of Real Estate Boards, with its cant about a Property Owner's Bill of Rights, and its real purpose, which was to keep race prejudice legal in all matters of the control of land. From our present standpoint it will be wise to resist this particular emotional satisfaction. Whatever feelings may stir others, the case for stronger government is not advanced by thoughts of revenge on anyone. It is justified in this instance solely and simply because we have accepted a particular goal as indispensable to a good society—the elimination of race prejudice—and because acts of government are indispensable to that purpose. We are not interested in punishment; the national guilt is at once too deep and too diffuse for that. We are interested in change. Moreover, I should notice here in passing what I shall have to discuss later—that there is a very wide distance between asserting to ourselves that we know it is right for our government to act against prejudice, and getting such action taken. We may well be asserting, in this case, something the American people as a whole do not yet believe, and we shall have to take fair account of this difficulty.

But the dangers of emotionalism and the difficulties of winning public support do not change my own conviction on this matter. We are rich enough, and we can be decent enough, to end poverty and racism. We can do it by action as a whole nation, and in that national action we shall need federal law and federal money—in short, federal government for freedom.

* * * *

The subject of communication is more subtle and less massive than that of race and poverty, and the notion of stronger government is open to a more attractive attack. When we look at the means of communication, we encounter all the real and powerful arguments against excessive governmental activity which are suggested by the magical words "free enterprise." And when we look at the content of what is communicated we encounter the still more magical words "free speech." It is true that the sensitivity of the communications industry tells something of its own awareness that the invocation of these great concepts may be something less than a complete defense against the case for stronger government. There is also something strange and interesting in the degree to which this industry reports on everything but itself. This is true generally: broadcasters do not discuss broadcasting and newspapers pay little attention to newspapering. It is still more true specifically: NBC does not report the doings of NBC, and *The New York Times* tells us very little about *The New York Times* (the irreverent but obvious question is whether conceivably the news about the Times is not all fit to print).

But while it is easy to poke fun at this industry, we have to begin by recognizing that the magical words have a basis in reality. The fact that abuses are committed in the names

14   of free enterprise and free speech does not make those notions wrong. I do not find it hard to agree that in this country A. T. & T. is a better instrument of communication for all than it would be if it were nationalized, and what is most seriously wrong with *The New York Times* is that there is only one of it. I am sorry that the men who run commercial broadcasting have come to think of it as an "industry" when it is necessarily so much more, and I regret the degree to which money talks more than mind throughout the field. Still there is no remedy for these troubles in direct government control. Freedom of enterprise and freedom of speech are among the freedoms a good government must serve.

So in this case it is quite a special kind of strength that I am asserting as necessary. I am not talking about using the power of the government to do what is better done by others, but rather about necessary increases in quite traditional—and even inescapable—functions of regulation, together with some modest but highly important activities which cannot be handled by private enterprise alone because they won't make money. To put it still more simply, we are at the early stages of an explosion in this field which is creating needs which only government can meet.

The most powerful element in this explosion is technological. Within this generation we shall certainly see changes in our capacity to communicate information greater than all that has happened since the invention of the telegraph. Whether by satellite or laser beam or both, whether by something like a computer or by something like a TV set or something like a telephone, or something related to all three, we shall be able to put all sorts of information in all sorts of places in ways that we quite literally have not dreamed of till now. If you greatly multiply the number of available channels over the eighty-odd that are now potential on TV, then give many of them a two-way capability, and add the capacity to reach essentially unlimited amounts of data, you can see that the living room can readily become a place with the combined advantages of a great research library and the total information net of the press, business, and government. It may be that we shall "borrow books" by tuning in on the Public Library channel, or that we shall do our shopping by two-way TV and pay our bills the same way. On other channels we may conduct serious scientific meetings without ever leaving our rooms.

I recognize that these extraordinary possibilities can carry a kind of terror with them. Probably many of you do not want this kind of instrument—or think you don't. You are in decent company; one thinks of Clarence Day's Father and the early telephone, or the average intellectual and present-day television. But in the world of technology what *can* happen usually *does* happen in one form or another—especially if it provides economic rewards. The real question is not whether changes of this sort are coming; they are inevitable (although of course there is wide room for error in the choice of illustrative samples of specific possibilities). The real question is whether things will be done well or badly, from the standpoint of our purpose of freedom. A simple example of a necessary requirement, from this standpoint, is that the owner of the instrument should retain the power to turn it

16   off (which is a power we can have, and which very few of us exercise, in the case of the telephone).

The limited and enormously valuable spectrum of radio frequencies has required at least a small amount of regulation for fifty years. Now that the possibility of varied uses has wildly expanded, this minimum requirement leads to major questions of national policy: the desires of military men against those of the private sector; the problem of interference, and so of priority, between television and telephones; the rights and wrongs of marginal infringement on the airwaves of neighbors—and so on until one inevitably reaches such a fundamental question as the comparative value of entertainment and education. The government did not create this explosion, but the explosion engages the government whether it will or not. For the government not to act, in such a case, is as big a decision as to act.

No one knows today just what way of arranging these things will be best, or even how to make that decision. For the present, indeed, one of the main tasks of government may be simply to prevent the foreclosure of important questions by decisions that time may prove to be unwise. I myself believe that a good example of such a role for government is to be found in the case of the attempt of the Communications Satellite Corporation to win recognition as the sole authorized operator of domestic communications satellites. The economic advantage of such recognition to COMSAT is self-evident, but nothing else about the problem is self-evident at all, and in particular it is not clear that there is compelling reason here to give up the well-known advantages of competition in favor of a licensed monopoly. Yet only a series of accidents led to the presentation of alternatives which have so far kept the door open for a more carefully considered national decision. The government needs more strength here.

A host of unanswered questions will have to be resolved as these extraordinary instruments become possible. Are we talking about a new kind of common carrier, or is it better to conceive of such an information service as a form of free press? What is the place or places for competition here? How far can there be provision for kinds of information that are usually regarded as matters for philanthropy or public service? Should such a system or systems be directly assimilated to the processes of public education, and if so, how are the economics of both the system and the schools affected? What about governments as consumers of this information, as well as regulators? To ask these questions is not to assert that government alone should give all the answers. An explosion of such enormous meaning will generate its own new forces which will affect the answers, and it is obvious that many existing companies and institutions will have the deepest interest in the outcome. All I am saying here— and it is quite enough for my purpose—is that the government must not be absent from this field of action.

The first role of the government will be regulatory. I see no reason to suppose that the government should move directly into general operation of such public systems on any large scale, though it may well wish to operate separate systems of its own, as for military communications. But,

18   as I shall argue in the next chapter, the regulatory role itself requires kinds of strength and skill the government does not now have.

Beyond the regulatory role there are limited but important needs for government action when the profit motive fails. The most conspicuous present case is the cause of Public Television. Twenty years of experience have made it very plain indeed that commercial TV alone cannot do for the American public what mixed systems—public and private— are offering to other countries, notably Great Britain and Japan. This case has been loudly argued in the last two years, and it needs no repetition here. The problem of combining federal support with independence from political pressure is a hard one—harder in our society than in either Great Britain or Japan. The Public Television Act has been passed and signed, but in early 1968 there was still no money even for its beginnings, and no agreed plan for long-range financing of a protected sort. But the fact that it is hard to do does not make it unimportant.

A more subtle task for the government is to find the right way of supporting public-service research in communications. Private enterprise, to its great credit, has performed prodigies of technological inquiry, and the explosive possibilities I have sketched owe their imminence to the mutually reinforcing connection between basic science and applied technology which is one of the greatest achievements of our society. But we have not made the same kind of investment in the analysis of these systems from the point of view of the general welfare—nor have we yet begun to experiment with imagination and energy on the possibilities for learning which are implied. It is good that a number of lively firms are trying to find their own ways to connect what they call hardware and software on a profitable basis, but I have the strong impression that the field is as difficult in the short run as it is promising, and the extraordinary importance of the public interest here suggests the same need for governmental funding of both basic research and promising experiments that has been crucial to other kinds of scientific progress.

To indicate the range of possibilities—and not to claim that early results are inevitable—let us consider, first, the attitudes of preschool children toward TV; second, the critical social value of a real headstart in reading; third, the talent that commercial television uses to hold the children's interest; and fourth, the vast amount of money our educational system now spends to teach reading. Taken together these considerations suggest the possibility that a few tens or hundreds of millions of dollars for research and development in preschool TV teaching might give a lot of our children a built-in headstart that would repay the investment in every possible manner. This may seem a dangerous idea in a number of ways; it might seem to take kids away from cereal ads and jobs away from teachers. But in reality children will still need both cereal and teachers, especially teachers. A very small start on these possibilities is beginning this year in a workshop financed about half and half by the government and by private foundations. This sharing is all very well at the present experimental level of three or four millions a year, but I suspect that when such programs be-

20   come generally attractive, they will call for financing on a scale which necessarily will require mainly governmental money.

Sooner or later, of course, the successful TV teaching of reading—precisely because it would offer such enormous practical advantages—should be at least as attractive, commercially, as the sale of textbooks to public school systems. The role of government in this case needs to be no more and no less than its role in supporting research for national defense, and in buying the results. Indeed the necessary and proper decentralization of responsibility for educational investment should make the federal government much less important than it is in the aircraft industry. All I am saying is that the government has a special pump-priming role to play before the laws of supply and demand take over. In this sense the role I propose is not only parallel to the modern partnership between government and industry which provides for the common defense; it is as traditional and conservative as the grants of land that helped build our railways and the agricultural experiment stations that have helped make the modern American farm.

*   *   *   *

Nuclear energy is a somber subject. Whatever may be its constructive possibilities—and they are very great indeed—what is dominant and even decisive about nuclear energy is that it can end modern society overnight. The business of preventing that catastrophe is everyone's business, and the indispensable instrument of that business is government. This, of course, is not a new notion—we are now in the

twenty-fourth year of the nuclear era—but I press it nonethe-
less as one of my three illustrations of the need for government because its overriding importance has a heavy impact on
the shape of government as a whole and also because it
seems to me that we do tend to forget it from time to time,
or at least to take it for granted in a way we never should.
Other great and pressing questions will come and go, but
there will be no escape from this one, and all the evidence
suggests that its impact upon government is much more likely
to grow than to decline.

From the very beginning, it is only fair to say, most Americans have understood the awful meaning of this new force.
No one who studies the record of the first few years of the
atomic age can fail to feel again the sense of horror and of
concern which gripped all but the most insensitive of those
who shared in the responsibility of the first decisions—which
is not to assert that all those decisions were perfect. The
creation of the Atomic Energy Commission reflected a sober
sense that this enterprise was so far beyond the ordinary range
of the merely military that it must have a special kind of
essentially civilian management. But of course the military
interest, and the military responsibility for defense, were not
ended by the new institution. It would be more accurate to
say instead that at best the Atomic Energy Commission pro-
vided an alternate channel for responsible concern, one in
which the view of soldiers would not automatically predomi-
nate.

The military role remained, and I am not one of those who
are disposed to criticize military men for their insistent
concern with the possibilities of nuclear weapons. What

22   else was and is their duty? The precise center of the nuclear
dilemma is that the existence of this weapon does require
strength as well as restraint.   Nor can it be said that the
military judgment has been wrong in all of the great debates
that have punctuated the history of the nuclear age in Washington. It seems clear now, for example, that the decision
to proceed with the hydrogen bomb was right; the Russians
had already made their own decision; we would have had
to follow them in any case, and no sober interest would
have been served by seeming to be caught flatfooted. But
my point, for the present, is not really who was right or wrong
in any one case. It is rather that by its very nature the explosive force of the nucleus has required a series of decisions of
the greatest gravity which can be made only by government.   Whether your object is unilateral disarmament or
unlimited military development, there is no escape from the
fact that what you are trying to affect is what the government does. I am not asserting that you have to be a part of
the government in order to play an effective part in this
process.   A number of individuals—Hans Bethe comes to
mind—have played notable constructive parts in this saga
without holding full-time government office, though most of
them have had access to information and to influence which is
much harder to have if you choose to stand apart entirely.
The problems of security classification and clearance, some
necessary and some not, have seriously handicapped the
outsider in this field. Yet he has a role and importance which
I do not wish to diminish—indeed I believe his role should
grow and not decrease. But my present point is more limited:

outsider or insider, soldier or civilian, scientist or moralist, pacifist or militarist, all of us come to this enormous set of dangers and choices as dangers and choices to be faced by the government.

Nor can we responsibly pretend that somehow the great decisions are behind us. In the cool comfort of the aftermath of the Cuba missile crisis of 1962 there was a tendency to suppose that somehow the final corner had been turned. This point of view was especially conspicuous in Europe, but it was not absent at home, and it was somewhat strengthened by our natural and justified delight in the Test Ban Treaty. Indeed, it is certainly true that one corner was turned, and we cannot doubt that the world has been less dangerous in the last five years because of what President Kennedy did for peace in those terrible two weeks. But the bombs and missiles have not gone out of existence. They have continued to multiply in number and in destructive power—and what is more serious still, the number of their owners has also grown. Now we are in the middle of another complex and demanding set of decisions on the development and deployment of still another massive nuclear weapons system. The problem may have been pushed into the background for a while. It did not go away.

What brings this point home to me, perhaps even more than the emergence of additional nuclear powers and demands for additional weapons systems, is that these terrible and necessary instruments are there every hour of every day. For most of us they may naturally and properly escape into the background most of the time, but this can

24   only be right if they remain in the very foreground of the daily attention of tens of thousands of other men. The systems of safeguards which are designed to give us both alertness against attack and protection against accident are not inhuman—they require men. Those men are a part of government. Without some confidence in them not one of us could responsibly turn to any other problem at all. There will be need for them, and for unremitting excellence in their performance, as far ahead as any of us can see. There will also be continuing need for a process of government in which they and we can continue to believe. No weak government can control the bomb indefinitely. This conclusion has alarming consequences in the field of foreign affairs, but here I am content to assert its relevance to the Government of the United States.

*   *   *   *

I have now made my first point to my own satisfaction, and while you may think I have indulged in overkill, in a way I am struck by my restraint. I could give a lot more examples of the need for government action. One which is especially close to my own heart is population control. The two great edges of advance in this field are biological research and public information—research so that a man and woman may come to have really cheap, safe and effective means of making their own choices—and information so that all grown men and women may have the same understanding of their rights and opportunities that is available to the educated and the affluent. For any government to force the choice of birth control on people would of course be a grave infringement of personal freedom, but not to set them free to make that choice for themselves is even worse. The necessary research is expensive, and the necessary programs of information and advice are more expensive still; so the government once again becomes the necessary instrument of action.

And beyond population I think of the economics of health, the conservation of resources, the rationalization of the laws governing transport and agriculture, and the problems of public and private education. I think even of foreign affairs, which I have put aside on special grounds. Let us take it for decided that there is plenty for government to do. It remains to consider whether there are any weaknesses in the government's capacity to do these things, and what there is that any of us can do to help.

2

Alarming Weakness

I have now explained my belief that we face a growing need for effective governmental action, and I have offered as illustrations the problems of race and poverty, communications, and nuclear explosions. Now I propose to argue that our existing system of government is already dangerously weak in relation to its present task. The obvious conclusion to this line of argument is that the government needs a double dose of reinforcement—first to meet its present responsibilities and second to meet the new ones that are coming.

I rather hope that these assertions cause great annoyance to some of you and some annoyance to nearly all. A residual mistrust of government is a necessary and desirable part of the American make-up. At the same time I also hope for your sympathy and even your agreement, in the end. So before we enter the second stage of the argument, it may be useful to pause for a brief look at this problem of our resentment of the claims of others for the virtue and strength of government.

There are aspects of it that are clearly good: for example, it is entirely right to require a practical demonstration of need before the government is authorized to act—and equally right to hold the government continuously accountable for what it actually does. Moreover, officials of government, like other human beings, find it easier to remember their powers than their obligations, and advocates of particular

30   programs can only too easily sound like greedy power-grabbers. My own support for greater governmental power is based on the belief that the case I advanced in such sketchy form can be defended in detail against the most searching cross-examination, and second on my expectation that all programs would be operated with a full accountability to the public. In this second assumption I specifically include the nuclear problem, where the real but limited requirement for some secrecy in details is not a necessary or desirable barrier to such public accounting. Whenever any power is sought for government, it is right to require that the need be real and that the power be accountably used.

I emphasize these simple points because they are often neglected in discussion of the general questions of the powers of government. Americans readily assume that the only way to prevent the abuse of power is to make sure that power does not exist. We are much too quick to quote Acton on the corrupting tendencies of power, and too slow to remember that Acton, the great friend of Gladstone, was writing out of an almost automatic acceptance of the need for government and for the purpose of showing how to make its exercise consistent with liberty.

This disposition to regard all political power as bad is indeed what is wrong in the instinctive reaction I hope you may have felt. Both logically and psychologically it begs such real questions as need and accountability, and it has the further unattractive aspect that very often those who surrender to it have quite a lot of private power of their own. I do not think the reaction of hostility to all public authority is usually insincere or cynical, even when it comes from men with such private power. But I do think that the

apologetics which have been used to piece out this combination of prejudice and self-interest are a discredit to our national dialogue—whether they come from Real Estate Boards, or organized medicine, or even student newspapers.

A further error in our thinking about political power is the assumption that strong government is inconsistent with strong private institutions and strong personal freedom. My own belief, which for now I assert without proof, is that within basic constitutional constraints the truth is much more nearly the opposite: that free enterprise, free competition, free universities, and free expression all *require* clearer and stronger political authority. It seems almost self-evident—to take some simple examples—that the free enterprise system is stronger today because of the New Deal, that the present economic powers of Washington are an indispensable part of the national prosperity, and that the current strength of our free universities owes a great deal to governmental support whose presumed dangers have proved grossly exaggerated. And conversely, I believe that when government is fractionated and subdivided—out of fear, or special interest, or simple inattention—it can come to be a burden upon our freedoms. This can happen either because government is weak in serving our basic needs, as in public education, or because it has become increasingly unaccountable, like the military establishment before McNamara, or for both reasons, as in the case of welfare.

So it is good to insist on need and accountability, and bad to react with hostile clichés that beg the question and obscure the real problem. But there is a more complex and interesting

32   reaction with which I feel considerable sympathy, namely the resentment we feel at any enlargement of the powers of government because somehow that only adds to what "they" can do to "us." I find this reaction in myself when I read bold new programs written by others. Even if I agree with their proposals, I find myself wondering who these people think *they* are. This reaction becomes still stronger if I find that what they mean to do is to use the government to change the way people behave, which of course is exactly what I have already said was necessary in my own remarks about race prejudice. If I am irritated by my own argument, I must at least recognize that there is a problem.

And indeed there is. We live in a world where for all sorts of reasons "they" tend to become more and more powerful while "we" become more passive. "They" make the things we buy, the news we read, the rules we work by, and the programs we see. "They" run the schools and colleges; "they" threaten our privilege or prevent us from having the power we deserve. "They" are usually faceless, and the government, even more than other sources of action, can only too easily be—or seem to be—a hostile and distant "they." As we urge that it needs more strength, we must keep this danger in mind. The danger will not be removed, though it may be greatly mitigated, by the most plainly demonstrated need and the most scrupulous accountability. We shall need something more, and for the moment let me say simply that I think the essentials of the answer will be found in the concept of the sharing of these new powers, so that somehow we get less power *over* and more power *with*—less power that is uniquely theirs and more that is somehow ours as well.

*   *   *   *

The American system of government is today far too weak to do the job now assigned to it, let alone the job that it ought to be given. I believe that this proposition is as true at one level of government as at another and as true of the legislative and judicial branches as of the executive, but I content myself with a discussion aimed at the Executive Branch of the federal government. The Executive Branch in Washington is probably the most important of all. It is certainly the one I know best. It is also the branch of government which is most frequently accused of excessive powers, and therefore if I can make a tolerable case that it needs reinforcement, the reader may be willing to accept, at least for argument, the notion that there may be a parallel need at the state and local level.

The simplest demonstration of the weakness of the Executive Branch is its current lack of adequate authority in matters of appropriation and taxation. Not only does the Executive Branch need Congressional approval for all its moneys and all changes in the tax rules—this much is both constitutionally necessary and politically desirable—but between them the Congress and the Presidency are so hobbled that neither one has effective authority except in the most unusual moments. Overinterpreting occasional short periods of great Presidential ascendancy, like the year 1965 or the early years of the New Deal, our public opinion tends to neglect (as Presidents never can) the fact that these moments of

34   executive freedom are rare in all fields and especially rare in the field of money bills.

Fortunately for my present purpose, though not for the present state of the union, there has been a classic instance of this perennial difficulty in this very year. In August of 1967 the Executive Branch reached a clear decision that the country needed increased taxes, and from that time forward the central business of the Executive Branch was to try to get action on this need. It is a pardonable exaggeration to say that throughout that period the convictions of Congressman Wilbur Mills had more influence on the programs of the Executive Branch than the convictions of President Johnson. In part this may have been the consequence of the fact that the President himself lived for a generation in Congress, where he naturally learned to think that the pending business on the Hill was the pending business of government as a whole. But even if Mr. Johnson had never been in Congress, the Executive Branch would have needed a tax increase very badly in 1967–1968; it would still have had to go to Congress to get it, and it would still have found Wilbur Mills in the chair of the House Ways and Means Committee.

I must make it clear that I intend no personal criticism of Mr. Mills. Obviously I disagreed with him on the urgency of the tax action, but if there is a Congressman of higher general ability and character, I do not know him. In using his power to the limit to serve the purposes he thought right, Mr. Mills was simply doing what we must expect any determined politician to do—indeed what we must want him to do. It is not the strength of Mr. Mills but the weakness of the whole government that I am complaining of. Mr. Mills himself, while he had great negative powers, was quite unable to substitute any great affirmative discretionary authority for that which he and his colleagues denied to the President.

Nor can I be put off by suggestions that the delay was the consequence of the special situation created by the war in Vietnam. Certainly Vietnam is a special case, but if the President's Great Society Program had been properly funded we would have needed new taxes in any case, and it is far from clear that the existence of a war makes a tax increase harder to get. In any case, there is nothing unique about long delays, and even decisive defeats, for the taxes and appropriations requested by the Executive Branch. The tax cut of 1964 was first sought by President Kennedy in 1962, and the weight of expert opinion is that it should have been sought still earlier. All that is really unique about tax policy is its critical importance for all aspects of the work of government.

Flexible tax rates are now quite simply indispensable to the effective management of economic policy—and so to strong and stable economic growth. The use of drastic changes in the interest rate as a total substitute is not only disturbing and wasteful in general, but especially destructive to the orderly growth of housing, which in turn is absolutely critical to the struggle against racism and poverty. Our government cannot meet its present responsibilities effectively —it cannot serve the whole economic system, public and private alike—it cannot avoid boom and bust—if it cannot

36   change basic tax rates, perhaps up to twenty per cent in
either direction, with much greater speed than our system
now permits. The Congress is too big and slow and varied to
exercise this power on its own. It should therefore delegate
that power to someone, and the President is a better agent
than any one Congressman, however honorable and able.

I am aware of the risk that this may sound like rampant
Caesarism, and I too have heard that the power to tax is the
power to destroy. But what we are talking about here is
nothing so drastic as a general abdication of Congressional
responsibility. We are talking about a legislative delegation
of discretion to move tax rates within relatively narrow
limits (and without changing the basic structure of the tax
system) in accordance with the best available judgment of
the nation's economic situation. This is a power very much
smaller than that which belongs to almost every other
English-speaking government in the world, as long as it has
a small Parliamentary majority. It is a power whose need is
overwhelmingly clear, and for the exercise of which any
President can be held fully and directly accountable by the
voters. Even a most superficial knowledge of the motivations
of Presidents permits the confident assertion that the constraints of democratic accountability will be ample, in this
field, to prevent any unreasonable upward use of such limited discretion. All politicians rightly hate to increase taxes
except when they have no other choice, and all Presidents
are politicians. The fact that this discretionary authority will
be very hard to get is irrelevant to my present purpose. In
tax policy the Executive Branch is not much too strong, as the

disbelievers in modern government tell us, but much too weak.

*   *   *   *

The Executive Branch is also dangerously weak in its own internal capacity for sustained, coordinated, and energetic action. In many areas it more nearly resembles a collection of badly separated principalities than a single instrument of executive action. Presidents Kennedy and Johnson have done more than most of their predecessors to assert and maintain executive control within the Executive Branch, but I think they would be among the first to recognize how much is left to do.

The unending contest between the Presidency and much of the bureaucracy is as real today as ever, and there has been no significant weakening in the network of triangular alliances which unite all sorts of interest groups with their agents in the Congress and their agents in the Executive Branch. My half-educated guess is that specialists in public administration might even say that the progress made by Presidents Kennedy and Johnson has been significant only where the network was relatively weak, as in the conduct of diplomacy, or where there has been an administrator of truly exceptional force and skill, as in the case of Secretary McNamara.

The familiar power of vested interests is worth closer attention by the consideration of a specific case, but first let me emphasize the simple point that the Executive Branch remains woefully short of first-class executive agents of the President. I intend no criticism of individuals. The trouble is

38   at the Cabinet level of the government, but it derives overwhelmingly from the present nature of the office and not from
the nature of the men who have occupied it. Obviously some
men do better than others; some Presidents use their Cabinet
officers more effectively than others; some of the Cabinet-
level jobs are more workable than others. But by and large
what is wrong is that the Cabinet office is still not understood,
at all levels, and by all hands, as truly Presidential in its character and power. As a result even very good Cabinet officers
tend to become special pleaders at the White House for at
least some of the interest groups that are strong in their departments. They find it hard to keep it steadily in mind that
they have a much greater and more important responsibility,
which is to help to frame and execute the policies of the Executive Branch as a whole.

In making this large claim for Cabinet-level office, I am not
trying to import Cabinet government. That notion, so full of
intellectual interest to students of comparative government,
is merely romantic when one considers the realities of the
American Presidency. Our Executive Branch has no place
for collective responsibility. Nor am I trying to reopen the
stale contest between Cabinet officers and the White House
staff—a battle more violent in the eye of the beholder than in
the reality of day-to-day life, at least in my experience. There
is plenty for the White House staff to do, but members of that
company seldom mistake themselves for Cabinet officers.
The Cabinet role which I am trying to describe is something
quite different. In its relation to the White House it must be at
once highly autonomous and deeply responsive. It is politi-

cal, but only in the President's interest. It is managerial, but only on the President's terms. The Cabinet officer must certainly be attentive to his departmental business, and he should seek to ensure that the President has timely notice of the impact of other policies on his department's specific interests, because the President needs to know when one of his oxen is about to gore another. But a Secretary should never choose his departmental interest as against the wider interest of the Presidency. At a test—unless he means to resign—the Secretary should always be the President's agent in dealing with the bureaucracy, not the other way round.

The basic argument for this kind of Secretary is simply that no other instrument can give the Presidency control over its own branch of government. The ablest of Presidents, with the most brilliant and dedicated of Executive Office staffs, simply cannot do it alone. The President has to have, out in each of the great departments, a group of men—with a leader—who are clearly and continuously his agents. Nor is it anything but a pale substitute to have these men at a level below that of the Cabinet officer himself. The historical record is full of examples of the trouble and frustration for all concerned that can come from the oh-so-skillful insertion of a President's man into the second or third level of a department. The place for the President's man, in every department, is at the top. And he should not be there alone and unattended; he needs a group of principal assistants, and an immediate staff, who see themselves as his colleagues in the business of acting for the Administration on the departmental scene. To put it another way, the "Presidential Appointment" must really be Presi-

40   dential, and it should be understood on all sides that it is nonsense to ask any man to accept executive responsibility for any of the great departments and then not provide him with a staff which will do for him, after its fashion and in its smaller scale, what the President's staff has been learning to do for him.

This is far from the present concept of the Cabinet, I admit. It leaves little room for the routine selection of geographically distributed political supporters, and it certainly does not permit the claim by any interest group that it has a prescriptive right to control the choice of a Cabinet officer. Indeed so sweeping is the notion of a Cabinet of real Presidential executives that very often when students of public administration are rearranging the Executive Branch to their taste, they content themselves with the proposal that the President be allowed a couple of Super-Secretaries, leaving the existing special-interest Cabinet offices in being. This might be a workable beginning, and the preliminary outline of such a position can be seen in the present office of the Secretary of Health, Education and Welfare. But it would be only a beginning, and I think we shall find that more is needed.

Obviously it will be hard to find the men for these jobs. It is always hard to find first-class executives, and the requirements on such executives in Washington are heavier and more varied than anywhere else in our society, except perhaps in half a dozen of the toughest assignments as mayor or governor. Certainly there can be no automatic assumption that success in other kinds of management means success in Washington. Moreover it will not be easy to get the Congress to provide the necessary support for such strongly staffed and clearly Presidential executives. We have fresh before us the cold reception that met the President's proposal of 1967 to merge the two most notorious special-interest departments—Commerce and Labor. Still I believe that the men can be found, and that some time in the next few years the necessary support can be built.

Some very good political analysts are nostalgically friendly to the traditional concept of the Cabinet; one of the best has complained to me about my neglect of the justification, in history and practice, for this traditional view. The point compels respect. Such analysts are right when they suggest that Cabinet officers who are not the President's men can still be politically convenient to him. They are also right when they emphasize that Presidents themselves often press the buttons of political commitment that set one Cabinet officer against another; in such contests the President will often meet himself on both sides of the contest. And finally, they are right when they insist that Presidents have made more trouble for Cabinet officers than Cabinet officers have ever made for Presidents. But this last point is my point too: it is the President, not the Cabinet officers, who has the right to make the trouble. There are certainly many obstacles in the path of the Cabinet officer who would seek to do his job in the way I am suggesting, and I am very far from suggesting that all of these obstacles can or should be ignored. Pressure groups have their proper as well as their improper claims, and Congressmen have rights and powers which deserve respect. But I insist on my contention that none of these forces should divert

42   a Cabinet officer from the fundamental loyalty he owes his President.

The most compelling example of the present need for stronger Cabinet-level government is in the struggle against racism and poverty. There has been no shortage of able, energetic, and dedicated men in this effort. They have faced a number of conventional problems of organizational overlap, and the program as a whole has suffered from over-selling and under-funding up and down the line. But what has also been wrong, above and beyond these difficulties, has been the absence of the clearly concentrated authority and responsibility which have become characteristic of the Defense Department in recent years. Short of the President himself, on question after question, there has been no one with the power to decide. Cabinet officers and the White House staff have made valiant efforts to resolve such questions without bothering the President—and President Johnson himself, like President Kennedy, has an extraordinary capacity for detail. But all concerned have been trying to make their own skill, energy, and good will serve as substitutes for the reconstruction of government which is increasingly required. I think they have had no other choice, given the mood of the Congress, but it is a safe prediction that the war against poverty will not be won until its high command in Washington is properly organized.

*   *   *   *

The absence of discretionary authority on tax levels and the inadequacy of the executive command and staff organization at the level just below the President may be the two most conspicuous present weaknesses of the Executive Branch, but there are two others of great importance which deserve our attention. They are the underrepresentation of the public interest and the inadequacy of the interconnection of parties with legitimate concerns. The first weakness can be illustrated clearly in the area of communications policy and the second in the field of nuclear weapons.

The federal body which is supposed to set communications policy for the nation is the Federal Communications Commission. Its weakness is a national scandal—which I do not take time to document here because the job has recently been done with unusual skill and insight by Elizabeth Brenner Drew, writing in the *Atlantic* of July 1967. Mrs. Drew makes it entirely clear that the commission is at present hopelessly outmatched as it attempts to make the rules that will ensure a fair deal for the public in a field where enormously strong commercial interests are quite naturally pressing their own economic advantage. The staff of the commission has traditionally had a high level of ability, but it is absurdly small because the Congress keeps it that way, and its range and effectiveness are further limited by the self-imposed regulations with which generations of commissioners have hobbled their own organization. Individual commissioners have had considerable ability and energy, but over the years the communications industry has had more to say than the rest of us about nominations to the commission. Moreover, members of the commission and its staff, even the most public-spirited, have shown a tendency to move on to the service of private com-

44   munications interests. In the circumstances it is quite remarkable that the commission has dealt firmly this last year
with the economic claims of A. T. & T., and it is not remarkable at all that it has failed to assert itself energetically on such
great issues of communications policy as those whose shape I
sketched so hastily in the preceding chapter.

The FCC is a regulatory commission, and it has the ambiguous relationship to both Congress and the Executive Branch
which is characteristic of such bodies. The Congress and the
Executive Branch in turn have an uncertain and somewhat
ambiguous relation to the public interest as distinct from the
special interests in communications. Individual Congressmen and Senators have a high degree of mastery of the subject, but many of them have commercial interests of their own,
many have had extremely quick and courteous service from
a common carrier in times of electoral need, and many are
sharply aware of the power of television in making and un-
making reputations. I do not mean to imply that the Congress
has been suborned by the communications industry; Congressmen and Senators as a group are more formidable and
more self-respecting than that. I do mean to suggest—and I
do not think most members of Congress would disagree—that
when there is a clash between public and private interests in
the field of communications, there is bound to be caution in
the Congress.

The Executive Branch has troubles of its own. In the first
place, as an extremely active user of communications, it contains powerful claimants both upon the wavelength spectrum
and upon other limited resources. The President has an as-

sistant for telecommunications who must keep clearly in mind the heavy claims of the Department of Defense. And in the second place, the Executive Branch just does not know quite where inside it the communications problem belongs. Recognizing this difficulty, the President in 1967 appointed a special committee of sub-Cabinet officers to advise him on some of the major immediate questions in this field—and the committee contains representatives from sixteen departments and agencies. The committee as a whole certainly has a strong concern for the public interest, but it must take careful account of special interests among its own members, and it is faced by the fact that its very existence demonstrates the absence of any continuing and stable center of executive concern with these issues.

Neither your patience nor my competence is sufficient to make this a good place for the solution of the problem of ensuring adequate representation for the public interest in a matter of this kind. It is a very hard problem indeed, not so much because of any special greediness on the part of the private or special interests concerned as because in the nature of things the concern of the rest of us ebbs and flows, while the well-paid attention of the representatives of carriers and broadcasters never flags for a moment. I think the building blocks of a solution lie somewhere in a combination of judicious amendment of the Federal Communications Act, substantial reinforcement of the FCC, and a quite explicit strengthening of the machinery of the Executive Branch.

It may also prove wise, in the end, to strengthen the connections between the commission and the Presidency. I

46   think Presidents would probably make better appointments if they were visibly responsible for the make-up of the commission as a whole. As it stands now, appointments come up one at a time, and for seven-year terms, so that there is no single moment at which the public or the President can effectively insist on a fresh start. Although I recognize that the terms of commissioners were made long and staggered in an effort to protect the commission from political pressure, I think it is doubtful that this kind of insulation has served the general welfare.

But particular remedies are less important to my argument than the fact of the disease. The reinforcement of the public interest in communications policy will not be easy to achieve, but the need is evident enough. That is all I want for now: a clear and striking case of imbalance between public and private interests. The case is unusually severe, but it is not unique.

*   *   *   *

The nuclear question illustrates many terrible and hopeful facts about our modern life, but none is more striking and interesting than what it has to teach about the difficulty of mutual understanding among different kinds of men coming at the question from different points of concern. This is a problem of great and growing significance in other parts of our life. One general consequence of the age of explosions is that it requires both special knowledge and understanding across the boundaries of that special knowledge. Nowhere is this more true than in dealing with nuclear energy.

The most critical of all the lines of connection here is from the scientist to the politician. From the days of Franklin Roosevelt and Vannevar Bush until now this process of communication has been of the highest importance. I will violate my own rule against reminiscence to say that I never admired President Kennedy more than for the combination of persistence and skill with which he sought scientific understanding and counsel, not only from his own outstandingly intelligent Scientific Advisory Committee, but also from others of varying opinions—and scientific opinion has never been unanimous in any major question of nuclear policy. President Kennedy made himself the master of their counsel, and he made them understand that his door was always open to them. This was not easy, especially as the President properly refused to give up his own final political responsibility for making such hard choices as whether to resume nuclear testing (he did resume it after Khrushchev did) and whether to forego a second series after Khrushchev had a second (he did forego it, and that decision led to the limited test ban treaty).

Yet even with close and clear communication at the summit, there have been difficulties between the scientist and the political leader. In President Kennedy's time, for example, there was a continuing problem (in which my own office may well have been the weak link) in maintaining adequate communication between scientific and political officers on issues of inter-allied nuclear policy. And in other Administrations there have been even graver breakdowns. The most tragic and destructive was the battle over the H-bomb, which led on to the attack on Robert Oppenheimer. Here a man of the

48   highest intelligence and the most profound patriotism was
        pilloried, partly because of the callousness of President Eisen-
        hower and the meanness of Lewis Strauss and partly because
        of his own tragic arrogance, but mainly because of a terrible
        failure of communication.

        The Oppenheimer tragedy recalls the importance, in nu-
        clear affairs, of the military. It was in the struggle over the
        hydrogen bomb that Oppenheimer exposed himself to danger,
        and it was supporters of strategic air power who were most
        outraged by his persistence. Ironically—and here we see the
        peculiar complexity of these contests within the Executive
        Branch—what outraged the air-power people most was Op-
        penheimer's almost clairvoyant insistence on the importance
        of tactical nuclear weapons in Europe. This was a problem of
        special interests as well as one of communication, and it re-
        mains hard for me as a civilian to feel sympathy for the tactics
        to which men of all services have descended, over the years,
        in their contests with each other—although it is only fair to
        add that the most passionate of all Oppenheimer's persecu-
        tors were not generals but civilian scientists.

        Yet my real point about the military in nuclear matters is
        not that they have contests with one another, but that they
        have found it so hard to communicate back and forth with
        others in the government about questions of weapons choice,
        strategic doctrine, and arms control. I have spent many days,
        in and out of government, wrestling with this difficulty, and I
        do not pretend to understand it fully. It is easy to be clever
        about the more irresponsible remarks of the less thoughtful
        military spokesmen, whether they are professionals like Gen-

eral Le May or amateurs like General Goldwater. What is
much more serious and much harder to understand is that
there has so often been great difficulty in communication between responsible civilians and the most sensitive and large-
minded of military men. I think what happens may be something like this: that the men who are striving to assess directly
military requirements have such a lot to do in staff analysis
and internal decision making that it becomes a full-time job
for them to frame a position that meets their own requirements. When they have gone through this painful process,
and made the adjustments and trade-offs which their internal
differences require, it then becomes very hard indeed for
them to reopen their own minds to the quite different points
of view that outsiders may have. It is much easier to fall into
the we/they habit of mind in which these outsiders become
adversaries to be overcome, not partners to be understood.
This tendency is somewhat increased by the fact that the military hierarchy is second only to the FBI in its distaste for candid staff-level interchange across bureaucratic boundaries.

But not all the failures are on the military side. We are
dealing with something deeper—with one aspect of the general problem of avoiding misunderstanding in an age of specialization. There have been similar failures of communication among others who have a special stake in nuclear
decisions. Those who are directly charged with seeking arms
control find it hard to talk not only with the military but also,
very often, with diplomatic colleagues who have the interests
of allies to consider. Those who have a particular commitment to the peaceful uses of atomic energy (they tend to be

50   dominant in the Atomic Energy Commission) do not find it easy to communicate with men who think that peaceful uses are of wholly marginal importance compared with the danger of nuclear proliferation.

This difficulty of understanding from one specialist to another is not unique to the nuclear field, although it may be uniquely important there. There are parallel difficulties in the field of communications and in the war against racism and poverty. Specialists are indispensable, but specialists who do not know how to talk to others outside their field are dangerous. Both in the nuclear field and in others, the American government has been relatively well served by experts working on their own problems, and relatively badly served by those, including the experts themselves, whose task it is to ensure that different specialists understand and respect each other's difficulties.

The nuclear case offers still another moral. The difficulties of communication within the government, grave as they are, seem modest and manageable when compared with three other problems of communication—with allies, with adversaries, and with the American people themselves. Skybolt and the Multilateral Nuclear Force remind us of the problem with allies, and the whole record of twenty years shows how hard it is to talk sense on these matters with Moscow or Peking. But consider for a moment the less recognized problem of the difficulty which our government has in talking with its own people, to whom it is directly responsible. In this case I am one who believes that the government has done reasonably well on the whole, but the need for effective work will be even greater in the future.

The crucial importance of public understanding of nuclear issues is often overlooked by students who are impressed with the obvious and awesome fact that the President as Commander-in-Chief has the sole and final authority to order the use of nuclear weapons. He does have this power, of course, but he has it in the context of two other enormous facts. The first is that, as President Kennedy once put it, the decision to use such weapons would be a terrible confession of failure. The second, which no President in the nuclear age has ever forgotten, is that he is the elected agent of the American people. The President necessarily knows much that the people do not know about the details of nuclear matters. But if the President and the people do not have a good mutual understanding on the basic elements of the problem, then the President is flying blind. It follows that there must be good communication from the government to the public and back again. The nuclear problem is not an example of some necessary and fatal disconnection between the government and the people, but rather a demonstration of the necessity that such communication be maintained. Certainly wise nuclear policy requires leadership from Washington, but equally certainly it requires public comment, public understanding, and, at moments of decision, public support. I have watched the nuclear decisions of this government reasonably closely, both from outside and from inside, since almost the beginning of the nuclear age, and I recall almost no instance in which a major decision has been made without a careful and generally accurate estimate of the harmony between that decision and the sentiment of the American people. On balance both the public and the government have dealt with this terribly dan-

52   gerous business in a reasonably sensible and farsighted fash-
      ion. If occasionally we have put too much faith in weapons
      and in megatonnage, we have still—on all the evidence so
      far—been the most nearly rational of nuclear powers. If occa-
      sionally the government has let its own logic outrun the judg-
      ment of the country as a whole—as in the case of the push for
      civil defense in 1961 (for which I have a share of respon-
      sibility)—still such departures from general public sentiment
      have been rare and rapidly corrected. And on the critical
      issue of arms control, while the government itself has too often
      been slow and unimaginative, it has still succeeded in sus-
      taining a national consensus in favor of accepting reasonable
      risks for this great purpose.

      Out of this national consensus has come a policy which,
      with all its troubles and risks, has kept the nuclear peace since
      Nagasaki. Our survival of the first twenty-three years of the
      nuclear age without a nuclear catastrophe and without sur-
      render to the nuclear power of others is one of the two great-
      est achievements of our national government in this genera-
      tion—the other being the more affirmative success of the
      sustained economic growth of the last seven years.

      A look at the future leaves little room for carefree optimism.
      The problem gets more complicated every year, and the task
      of communication between the people and their government
      grows correspondingly harder. If weapons systems continue
      to expand (and without a new level of understanding with
      our adversaries it is hard to see how such expansion can be
      avoided over the long run) and if efforts to achieve some form
      of arms limitation are intensified, as they surely must be, the

task of maintaining reasonable communication will grow. We will need progress in the interconnection of experts and specialists in and out of government. We will also need to strengthen the process of discussion and debate in Congress. But in the end (and here the familiar imagery is sound and right) the relation between the public and its government in nuclear matters is a problem for the President himself, in direct touch with the nation. So far there has been no major breakdown in this vital element of government, and the Presidential election of 1964, whatever else it means, surely underlines the national understanding that the clarity and soundness of this relation between President and people is vital to us all.

Still I hope you may be feeling that in the nuclear business the avoidance of breakdown is really not enough: that mankind must not be condemned to live forever under the Damoclean threat of nuclear apocalypse. I agree, although I must insist on Oppenheimer's chilling reminder that what man once learns how to do becomes a permanent part of his possibilities. Your insistence that we must do better simply strengthens my basic point. If we see this danger not merely contained, but reduced, in our lifetime, it will be through government—and through a government with greater strength for this purpose than the one we have now.

Indeed in these nuclear matters even the best and most subtle concern for the process of communication is no substitute for the other necessary elements of effective action. There must be something worth communicating, and both at the beginning and at the end there must also be authority. What

54   permits us to emphasize the need for communication in the nuclear case is that here, at least in theory, the decisive responsibility of the President is unquestioned. (I pass by the peculiar role of the Joint Committee on Atomic Energy, which would require a book in its own right; the Committee's leading members would agree, I think, that their own great role is still subordinate to that of the Commander-in-Chief, although they could properly point to many cases where they have had importance of their own.) Moreover the special problem of communication within the government tends to be harder or easier to solve as the President himself gives less or more attention to it. So far from being a substitute for effective strength, such good communication may be better understood as the consequence of a strength which knows enough to insist on getting the word, and getting it around.

When a President does create this kind of expectation, the federal government can show itself a lively and responsive organism. When they are assured of a fair hearing by the man who will decide, our public officials, both military and civilian, do much better work than our stereotyped expectations suggest. What is essential is that they should be led to do it.

I have done almost all I intend, now, to suggest that the government is not strong enough to do its business, and I have scattered a number of hints about the kinds of things that need to be done about it. In the next chapter I will try to be a little more specific, at least about the things that individuals can do, but first let me make brief comments on two very large questions which I have been skirting so far. They are the problem of the shape of the Presidential government and the problem of knowing just what the public interest is, in a pluralistic democracy. I have been talking as if the Presidency and the Executive Branch are, or should be, almost the same thing. I have also been assuming that somehow government can and should determine what the public interest is and then act accordingly. These are considerable assumptions.

Evidently I am one of those who believe in the power of the Presidency. Of course it is not the whole of the Executive Branch, and it should not be. Moreover, the President as an individual and the Presidency as an institution are not identical, though they are obviously inseparable. In arguing for extending the reach of the Presidency, I am not talking about extending the naked power of the President as an individual. The President who indulges his personal whims except in matters of no real importance is taking political risks which Presidents simply do not like to take. In this respect the combined constraints of politics and publicity are so heavy that there is a deep and fundamental difference between the power of the Presidency, even when it is strongest, and the powers of kings and emperors to which it is so readily compared.

I would argue, indeed, that insofar as there is a tendency to excessive personalism in the Presidency as it now operates, the right remedies are of the very sort I have been suggesting. Limited discretionary power over tax rates seems to me likely to decrease and not increase the risk of capricious and one-sided action at moments of change in economic climate. Increased prestige and authority for Cabinet-level executives should reinforce the Presidency, but it should also reduce both the need and the temptation for sudden interventions by the

56 President as an individual. It should also increase the number of men who are publicly and politically identified with the work of the Administration, thus increasing the role of others beside the President in the vital process of communication between the government and the public.

In passing let me add that I do not accept the frequently argued view that American Presidents, in necessary defense of their own prerogatives, must be resistant to the notion of strong Cabinet executives. The precise reason for the President to seek such powers for such officers is that they are among the very few people in all the government who are wholly answerable to him. His Attorney General, his Secretary of State, and his Secretary of the Interior are his men in the sense that can never be wholly true of leaders of the FBI, the Foreign Service, and the Bureau of Reclamation. Twentieth-century history shows no example of a successful attack by a Cabinet officer on his President, and if Presidents like Franklin Roosevelt have sometimes tolerated Cabinet members with whom they were out of sympathy and whose powers they kept clipped, this has been less because of well-placed political fear than because of an ill-placed belief that it didn't really matter. It did matter, and it matters more now.

Presidents have an evident right to be sensitive about loyalty, and their need for unswerving support from their Cabinet officers is made particularly intense by the fact that it is the President who has to face the voters. But in the relations between the President and his Cabinet it is to the advantage of all to follow the dictum of Henry L. Stimson—himself a great Cabinet officer—that one good way to make a man trustworthy is to trust him. No Cabinet officer will be perfect, and all will need Presidential guidance or correction from time to time, but if it is understood on both sides, from the first, that a Cabinet officer must be an executive agent of the Presidency, the odds on a sound relationship are good. The best example, after all, comes from an earlier time when the advantages of the President were much smaller than they are now—it is the case of Lincoln and Seward.

So I do not apologize to future Presidents for urging the reinforcement of the Presidency within the Executive Branch. The President of the United States is the most continuously watched and the most intensely accountable public official in the world. The Constitution, our tradition, and the public interest unite to make his office the right source of a new executive strength which he must share beyond his own staff.

Now let me suppose that you accept the argument so far— there is still the question of what the public interest is. In one sense of course it is foolish to try to answer in a few paragraphs a question that philosophers live with for a lifetime. But to neglect the question would be more foolish still, since it is central to the argument.

First let us grant that the Presidency can go wrong. Every great President has made serious mistakes, and nearly every President has seemed fundamentally wrong to some important sector of society. Expert counsel, effective control, and sound internal communications can help toward sound choices, but they cannot guarantee against error—and even very large-scale error. I have been a defender of the main lines of our Vietnamese policy, for example, but I certainly

58   do not contend that no mistakes have been made in that field.

Unfortunately the only certain guarantee against the misuse of power is to withhold the power, and by definition we are talking about powers which are needed for freedom. They can be limited by the terms of law; their use can be intensely observed; above all, in the case of the President, their user can be held accountable. But the power has to be conferred.

The public interest is what serves the freedom of all. But obviously the hard cases involve choices among freedoms. In this process of choice one can face questions of faith, questions of factual analysis, and questions of judgment on relative values. I hold it as a matter of faith, for example, that race prejudice is bad (I think I could prove it, but I believe it without proof). I hold it as a matter of factual analysis that there is no substitute for an open-occupancy law in combatting such prejudice, and I hold it as a matter of judgment that the freedom advanced by such a law far outweighs the unrestricted freedom in the sale and rental of real estate. To me, then, an open-occupancy law is in the public interest. And behind this sketch of a position is a whole series of opinions about what is wrong and what is right in our society, what will make it better and worse, and what is the relation between the individual and the society of which he is a part.

Let me outline my conviction in another way, by saying that often the public interest is that aspect of the question which we can see clearly only when our own particular interests are not involved. The public interest in lower tariffs, for example, is usually clear to a majority of those who are not seeking some particular protection for themselves, and in this case I think the majority is right. I also think that the public interest in questions of limited war may not be best discerned by those who are most directly affected, either by the rewards of battle or by its dangers.

I am far from asserting that the public interest is always and only what is opposed to some private or special interest. There is enormous value in the notion that the organized power of society exists to permit the realization of your private purposes and mine, and considerable force in the argument that society works well only when all its wheels know how to squeak and most of the squeaky wheels get greased. One of the reasons for confidence in the Executive Branch is that its elected chief is almost certain to have a lively sense of these proper private interests. If one were forced to a choice between some absolute notion of Public Virtue and the practical process of balancing out all special interest, I think it would probably be better to choose the latter.

But the balancing is not automatic, and a blind struggle among special interests is no prescription for the greatest happiness of the greatest number. Laissez-faire economics and pressure-group politics are equally inadequate as sovereign remedies. Both in economics and in politics there is need for a wider view of what is good. The unaided market place cannot even give us clean air or water. So it is fortunate that the notion of public interest is real to most Americans, and even better that the man in the White House, by all our traditions, has both the opportunity and the duty of proclaiming and serving that interest while he also attends to our private concerns. That Presidential obligation calls for still another kind

60   of leadership, above and beyond the operational need for authority which we have been discussing. There is no institutional or administrative reform which can give this kind of strength to a President. Most fortunately for all of us, the quality of imaginative concern for what America ought to be is what Americans have valued most in their Presidents, next only to the evident capacity to govern. The problem, of course, is to tell the real thing from the plausible fake.

But Presidents are not our last resort. In the end, we go beyond our belief in the public interest to a further act of faith by which we assert that questions about this interest are best resolved, directly or indirectly, by appeal to the electorate. We recognize the mix of public and private purposes which moves the individual voter, but we also suppose that the electorate can strike the balance—if not well, at least better than it can be struck in any other way. This assumption may well be larger and less provable than the prior assumption that such a public interest exists and that a President can play a unique role in defining it. But it is the necessary assumption of democracy, and we make it.

I think that we are right to do so. The American people have great common sense and an unusually strong attachment to the higher values of a free society. We also have a number of weaknesses, and one of them is an attachment to ideological stereotypes which makes us think we are more hostile to effective government than we really are. We have a strongly rooted preference for private systems of action, incentive, and reward—a preference I share. Like the government itself, our people can be wrong—and the public, like any individual, is often of two minds. You can get a majority to vote in favor of *de facto* race prejudice if you are a skillful expositor of traditional real estate attitudes; but you can also get a majority in favor of change if you can get people to see the issues in terms of the rights of all men as against the power of one group to keep another down.

You will observe that I am not engaged in anything remotely resembling proof. I am engaged, once again, in assertions supported by faith and illuminated by illustration. I believe that there is a public interest; I believe that on most issues it can be discerned by reasonable men and can win support from public opinion. I believe that in this process the government has a special responsibility, and while I have emphasized the Executive Branch, I think there is also a very great role here for the Legislature. You may say that I am an optimist, and so I am. My own almost instinctive belief is that our government can and will be reformed.

3

What You Can Do

The explosions of our age require stronger government. The government we now have exhibits many weaknesses. This is the two-sentence deposit of the argument so far. Now our business is to consider what we, as individuals, can do about it.

The actions I have to suggest fall in two main classes, acts of analysis and acts of participation, and I do not think one class is more important than the other. I address myself as to a university audience, though I hope what I say may be relevant to some who are older and younger.

The university audience, as I presume to define it for this chapter, is the generation of college and university people who are old enough to care about these questions of government and not so old that they have already clearly decided just what they intend to do about them in making their own choices of life. Most men and women still have a wide range of choice while they are undergraduates, and for several years after. Indeed my guess is that at any given moment during that period their choices are wider than they tend to think. One is not prevented from a career in science, for example, because one is behind in the orthodox progression of scientific courses, and one is certainly not blocked from medicine because he has neglected the prescribed requirements. A year's work—and often less—can repair that kind of damage, and a year is much less than the young tend to think. On

66 the other hand I do think that sometime in the late twenties the need for choice begins to sharpen. The passing years in the decade after graduation do tend to become a part of what a man is and a growing part in what he is likely to become. Freedom of choice is large in the twenties but much smaller in the thirties. "Your generation," then, might include most of those under thirty, and not most of those older.

So you are under thirty. I further assume that you choose to be a participant in government. You intend to conduct yourself so that for you the process of American government is not something "they" do but something "we" do.

This is not just a game with pronouns. It is a serious assumption about the present university audience. In my own time it was an assumption very few of us made in our college years—at least consciously. What I assume is not only that you will govern—that much is a simple necessity, as time passes—but that you intend to govern. If I am right, yours may be the first university generation for which this proposition holds generally, but then yours is the first—or perhaps the second—for which it is really necessary. Before the age of explosions Americans could reasonably leave the government largely to "them."

To intend to become a first-person part of modern government is of course presumptuous. The structure of human society being what it is, there are always more governed than governing. Moreover, even for those who do become active in the process of government, many parts of that process will always belong to "them." Presidents themselves—especially in their moods of "splendid misery"—have been known to find the world, and even the Executive Branch itself, more full of "them" than of "us." Your intention is not only presumptuous but necessarily partial. Both the presumption and the partiality deserve attention.

The first and best defense of presumption in expecting to be a participant in government is that in this country anyone else can do the same. It is enormously easier for some than for others, but no one can be left out entirely if he really makes the effort. One man's ambition does not of itself hold back any other man, and all the traditions of our society make such ambition legitimate.

So far so good, but not quite good enough. As you make this decision to participate, I hope you will make another: that when the process of government, or part of it, becomes "we," the majority which stays mainly outside that process will not become "they." The ideal, even for Presidents, is that all men should be our brothers, but the process of active politics involves plenty of disagreement and contest, and if Presidents see the world as full of "them," lesser men may be excused if they sometimes make the same error. My point is that at least you should not make this mistake in its elitist form—the form in which "we," the governors, know what is good for "them," the governed. Our society is Aristotelian, not Platonic; the interests and opinions of the citizenry, not the wisdom and rank of the governors, are the legitimating force of our politics. In presuming to join the process of government the best insurance a man can take out against arro-

68   gance is always to assume not only accountability *to* but sympathetic membership *in* that general public. A man may be able to do wonders *with* it—he can do very little *to* it.

This point is worth emphasis in addressing a university audience because arrogance is endemic in the academy. I have been accused of it myself and it is an accusation which is nearly always self-justifying, at least in part—so it always leads me to repent and sometimes even leads me to reform. It is not an attractive quality anywhere, and in politics it is exceedingly unhelpful. The rolls of our academic life have carried the names of distinguished men strongly inclined both to politics and to arrogance, and there may be one or two still around. Do not imitate them in their arrogance if you are serious about American political life; they try not to imitate themselves when they are really serious.

There remains a good and right way to imitate the political professors (and of course not all of them are arrogant, and none is arrogant all the time). They are profoundly right in their belief that ideas affect the action. Indeed I think that before the active politicians will be able to attack the kinds of problems I have been presenting, the political thinkers will have to do a lot more work. I have noted earlier, for example, that we are going to have a hard time using the power of government more energetically against racism as long as a working majority of all Americans continues to exhibit some degree of prejudice. There is here a task of political persuasion which the embattled politicians are not likely to do alone.

The politics of strong government—of authority and accountability—for which I have been pleading is a politics which really does not yet command the intellectual and emotional support of most of the people of our country. Except in the field of national defense, or at moments of special crisis, our people really do not think they believe in active government, and our politicians do not preach it either. The Jacksonian bias against authority remains the national mode even in a time when the vast majority of us have learned to rely on all kinds of specific federal programs. In a notable little book Free and Cantril have lately drawn our attention to the striking fact that on balance Americans are ideological conservatives and pragmatic liberals.* We can sympathize with the platitudes of a Goldwater, but we shiver when he seems to apply them to Social Security—and conversely, the ideology of the left in each generation continues to terrify us while plank after plank of the left-wing platform is being stolen by moderates in office.

We have lived that split life for a long time. Professors and public servants have learned much skill both in the analysis and the operation of a great government whose public posture must be that it really doesn't amount to much and whose operational powers are in fact far less than the public has learned to assume. It is tempting to suppose that executive feebleness of the sort I have tried to describe can be overcome step by practical step while the ideology of our government remains undisturbed. But my own belief is the opposite. If what I have been saying is right, the obvious task for all of us who care about taking part in a government which has

* Lloyd A. Free and Hadley Cantril, *The Political Beliefs of Americans*, Rutgers University Press, 1967.

70 strength is to make the case for the value of that strength to our countrymen. This is the very first thing that you can do.

* * * *

One way we could begin is to help our people see the Presidency in all its present imperfection. The glamor that surrounds our Presidents too often distracts us from the reality of their operational weakness. This distortion begins with our almost unending preoccupation with the election campaign, as distinct from the operation of government. The making of Presidents has become the most interesting of all our spectator sports. Even among those who have chosen to play a part in government it is very often a part in this process that seems most interesting. Theodore White gives us a brilliant account of this contest every four years, and there is no one who does a remotely comparable job on the still more important battle to make the Presidency work. Obviously there is a natural drama to the Presidential campaign which cannot be found so readily in the hard process of conducting the government's business. Our Presidential elections, with all of their confusion and complexity, have an inherent dramatic unity which is beguiling. Mr. White cannot be blamed for doing the best job of all in a process of observation and analysis that preoccupies our press, our television, our pundits, and even our political scientists.

Another distraction from the real business of government is the preoccupation with personality, with "image." Certainly for the average citizen there is a special aura that surrounds the Presidency itself. In at least one of its moods the public likes to take an Augustan view of the President; this was the mood of airport crowds, as I remember them, in 1963 and 1964, and it is a still easier mood for passengers on Air Force One and for guests at White House dinners. But it is a mood which is more personal than operational. It is more a part of what makes the White House a "bully pulpit"—which it surely is—than a solid underpinning for real executive authority, widely delegated and energetically used. No one had more of this sort of personal prestige than General Eisenhower, but unfortunately he had it partly because he did not use it much.

Thus in the minds of most of us the very splendor of the Presidency somehow tends to diminish its meaning as the center of management. Even the most knowledgeable and experienced of Washington observers are schooled to think of the Presidency and its surroundings in personal terms. The men are more discussed than their policies; the policies are more discussed than performance; and when performance is assessed, it is more often by the record of legislation passed than by the record of laws administered.

Presidents themselves, in the last twenty years, have plentifully contributed to the confusion of priorities. They come to the office as victors in the terrible contest of politics; they cannot think of that past as *only* prologue. They read their own press notices (too much, in my experience), and they know that in politics it is often the appearance which is the reality. They do not come into office, characteristically, with

72   any clear sense of the vast gap between the pre-eminence of the Presidency as a target of human ambition and its weakness as an instrument of government for freedom. So they do not do all they might to take charge of their own government; instead they too often *appear* to take charge of it and then find themselves defending the appearances. Both of the Presidents for whom I worked closely had to learn by experience how hard it was to take charge of their own branch of the government. (One of the advantages of a number of the candidates of 1968, in this connection, is their previous close experience of the frustrations, as well as the satisfactions, of Presidential power.)

But we should not blame Presidents too much. Their error is the error of academic and journalistic fashion too. The conventional wisdom does not hold that the Presidency lacks the strength it needs. This is not what most scholars of the Presidency have told their students, nor is it what the best of modern reporters tell the public. The standard view of the press is that the Presidency is too big for its britches; the standard view of the academy is that it is as big as a President makes it.

So if I am anywhere near right in my general assessment of the weakness of government, my first call must be for help in making the case, help from men who know much more than I do about the kinds of weakness of which I have given brief examples. We require something not far short of a new theory of government, but I have no such theory to propose. My ambition is the simpler and lesser one of awaking others to a task that needs doing. That task has been slighted for so long that it will take a long time to do it right. I shall be content to

suggest some propositions that have a claim to be accommo-
dated in any new theory. Not all of them are new.

* * * *

First and most obviously, the need for effective government must always be demonstrated case by case. Social Security and medical care are notable cases where visible need
has gradually overcome shibboleths, with help from both
analysts and politicians. This method can sometimes do the
job alone, and I have already made the point that without such
demonstrated need there is no case at all for governmental
power. So this argument is always necessary, and sometimes
sufficient.

A second relevant proposition about government is that,
even at its largest and most demanding, it still remains quite
small. With respect to the federal government at least, the
case here is very strong—and some of the more eloquent and
less noticed speeches of both John Kennedy and Lyndon Johnson have been devoted to it. This proposition is important
both because of the strong national bias against "big government" and also because in fact it would be bad if the relative
size of the federal government were to expand very much.
(A little later I will argue that *strong* government and *big* government are not at all the same thing.)

But the trouble with these two propositions is that they tend
to omit the hard fact that if the government is to do what needs
doing, the government must have adequate authority. The
two propositions are more negative than positive: they tell us
that we need medicare because otherwise older people will

74   suffer, and that we can risk it because the government really isn't so very big to start with. But such arguments say little or nothing about what will be needed to run the medicare program well. They leave plenty of room for the error we have made repeatedly in the last generation: we start the program, but we do not give its managers the instruments and the authority they need. This is a mistake we are currently making in such fields as public education and urban renewal. Or if at first we do give such powers (and it sometimes does happen that way, at first, because of a special sense of urgency and because the new programs may enjoy special favor in high places), then all too soon the brave new enterprise is subjected to all the suspicions and restrictions that apply generally to "the bureaucracy." This is a danger that now threatens the poverty program. In pressing the case for new authority in relatively timid and apologetic ways, we may even have hindered and delayed the necessary recognition of the kind of authority that is really required. If you are constantly explaining how small you are, and how modest your claims, it is not easy to turn around and say that you cannot do your job unless you get much wider discretionary power. Neither can a government which is excessively modest make much of a case for attracting first-rate servants.

So if any new theory is to be adequate to the new needs of the age of explosion, it must somehow be much more affirmative. It will have to make government not simply a necessity, but a virtue—as free enterprise is virtuous, or collective bargaining, or learning. If we want government to do its job, we must make government an object of honor.

As one element in this process, there must be major reinforcement of the powers of agents of the Executive Branch. I have argued this case already at the level of the Cabinet. Here as elsewhere we should make it the explicit rule, and not the undiscussed exception, that our public servants should have ample executive authority. To me the simplest and most straightforward demonstration of such confidence would be to establish pay scales and rules of appointment which will allow a senior governmental executive to get the men he wants. Let me indulge in reminiscence again to say that the one enormous advantage, in present-day Washington, of working in the White House is that if you cannot get the best men in the country to help you, it is your own fault. The White House staff is a better place for the relatively young man than for the middle-aged, but with that exception, a President and his chief assistants can have their choice. Although the pay is not high, the other compensations are sufficient. But there is only one White House, and I have already emphasized my belief that truly effective government, in the Executive Branch, requires quality, energy, and staff-work out in the departments. For that kind of Cabinet leadership we need salaries roughly twice the size of those which are now permitted—and also larger and stronger staffs.*

* Doubling the pay of a Cabinet officer, as of March 1968, would move his salary from $35,000 to $70,000, but it would change his take-home pay much less. Depending on his family circumstances—and the level of his private income, if any—the actual magnitude of the increase might vary from $10,000 to $20,000. Cabinet officers would still get no more pay, in real terms, than their predecessors of sixty years ago, who received 12,000 old-fashioned dollars, free of income tax.

76   Salaries and staffs, of course, are instruments, not ends. But we are an instrumental people, and we tend—no doubt too much—to value men by what we pay them and the topnotch help we give them. At the very least we can say that one sign of the coming of the necessary revolution in our view of the value of government will be a drastic upward movement in the pay, and in the staff support, of the government's senior executives. One major step forward was taken in 1967 when the Congress established a new Quadrennial Commission on salaries. This commission will make recommendations for top salaries in all three branches of the federal government, and its recommendations will take effect automatically unless the Congress acts affirmatively to overrule them. This delegation of authority will help to spare the Congress the unreasonable pain of seeming to raise its own salaries (which are also much too low). This is one small but significant example of a kind of legislative delegation of authority which is good for effective government, and I think it highly significant that the man who invented this new instrument was Senator Everett Dirksen.

But of course there is much more to government than decent rates of pay. Executives need release also from other current constraints: from laws so loaded with detail that discretionary responsibility is crushed, from patterns of power in which their nominal subordinates are in fact almost wholly autonomous, from legislative scrutiny which mistakes the trees for the woods, and even from the trivial Presidential intrusion which in the past has often been a necessary antidote to inertia or impotence.

Any reconstruction of our view of government will require a reconstruction of our view of those who govern. In that sense my emphasis on the need for an upgrading of Cabinet-level executives may be merely a special case of a larger need: that we should enlarge and elevate our view of all forms of public service. The image we have of "the politician" and "the bureaucrat" may have to change. Or if we prefer to keep the unfriendly edge of such words, for use on those who somehow fall short of their high calling, then we need to find and to use other words for those who do better. But I do not insist on terminological reform; it may well turn out that we are so much attached to our right to cock a snook at government that even while we upgrade our civil servants in fact we shall still be downgrading them in language—there is plenty of precedent for that sort of thing elsewhere in our society. What is important is not the language but the reality: the public service needs more honor among us.

Any new theory of the Executive Branch of the federal government must also be based on a repudiation of the old mechanical notion that any gain of power for A is a loss for B or C. There is no necessary conflict between the notion of strengthening the Executive Branch and that of strengthening the Congress. Congress today has great negative power and much excessive control over bits and pieces of the government. But in the general affirmative functions of a legislature it is not too strong but too weak. It is understaffed; it is badly organized; its collective reputation falls far below the merits of Senators and Representatives as individuals. It has allowed a multitude of small concerns to overshadow its national

78 business. That it works as well as it does is a tribute to the extraordinary abilities of scores of its members. A proper theory of modern government will make the Congress stronger, not weaker. This is not the place to write that theory, but there is one familiar element I believe it should include: a Congressional grant of the item veto at least on appropriation bills. That grant would take the Congress out of little things it does badly and force it back to the big things it does best.

The need for a stronger federal government is matched by the parallel needs of state and local governments. The vicious circle by which mistrust has imposed impotence on these lesser systems of political action must be broken. Not only is there no contradiction between strength in Washington and strength at the state house and in city hall—the three kinds of strength are in fact mutually indispensable. We must reorganize our thinking so as to understand this necessary partnership of effective power.

Still another requirement of a new theory of government is that it should take account of the fact that the strength of government can be a friend, not an enemy, to strong private enterprise. There is no greater fallacy in our political tradition than the assumption—so widely shared by both liberals and conservatives—that the only right relation between effective government and effective private enterprise is one of hostility. In my own experience most of the sillier notions on this subject are propagated from the right. Often they come from men who have little practical experience of the real connection between government and business, but there is also a much less forgivable tendency of sophisticated businessmen to cloak their own need for speical advantage behind a veneer of rhetoric about free enterprise. The communications industry, in the past, has been particularly prone to this sort of doubletalk, so that, for example, a franchise granted by the government becomes a right, and not a privilege. What has been true since the time of Theodore Roosevelt is still true today—that more effective government, at every level, is the friend and not the enemy of the strength and freedom of our economic system as a whole. This does not mean that government must be the silent servant of business, of course, and perhaps it is just here that special interests make their mistake.

Despite all the self-righteousness and narrowness of its loudest spokesmen, the American system of enterprise has been a great engine of freedom. Its survival and reinforcement is a proper major goal of policy. But the beginning of political wisdom for businessmen must be a recognition that the business world cannot survive at all if our system of government is not strong enough to do its part of the job.

At the same time businessmen and other Americans are entitled to government that does not confuse strength with size, or effectiveness with a passion to do everything itself. The error of confusing strong government with big government is common today among both those who tend to praise government and those who abuse it. But it is not the size of a man's agency or bureau that determines his effectiveness in government; anyone who has worked in Washington will know of intramural contests in which strength and size have been inversely related. This point can apply to money as well as personnel. I think it will turn out, for example, that rent

80   supplements can produce more results for fewer dollars, in the poverty war, than any other single instrument in the enormous field of housing; and in the long run I think the government's education laboratories, working with a few tens of millions, may do more for children who need special help than all the billions of grants to schools in Title I of the Elementary and Secondary Education Act (necessary though those billions surely are). A true reform of welfare is likely to bring smaller staffs and simpler processes, and in the long run even lower over-all costs. The overdue attack upon the size of our overseas staffs which has been stimulated by the balance-of-payments problem is quite likely to produce stronger as well as smaller embassies abroad. And a truly strong Cabinet-level executive may tend to want a smaller and not a larger bureaucracy around him.

More broadly still, when government does at last mount an effective attack on the modern shame of the cities, it may find that relatively low-cost incentives to American enterprise may be among its best instruments. We can make this effort rewarding to the entrepreneur if we seek out the right ways of doing it. There need be no more conflict between business and government in this effort than there is in the field of national defense—although the analogy reminds us that wherever you have a buyer and a seller you have a need for prudence on both sides.

But the most important element of all, in a modernized theory of government for freedom, may be the reconciliation of strong political authority with effective and widespread political participation. If strong government is to be government for freedom, and indeed if it is to be recognizably American, it must be reconciled with the difficult but fertile concept of "maximum feasible participation"—to borrow the language of the Poverty Law. This idea is difficult because in a mass society there are many forces that separate the authority of government from those whom it affects—and in the war on poverty these forces are intensified by the turmoil, the inexperience, and the disadvantages of education that the program aims in part to attack. But the idea is also fertile because out of it can come the kind of reconnection between government and the citizen which is indispensable to both freedom and democracy in our age.

I hold that there is no necessary contradiction between the concept of effective public authority and that of maximum feasible participation. If you want participation you must first have something to participate in, and the way to give a share of power to the people in these cases is first to give real power to an agency of government. I think the accountable executive is much more likely to afford real participation to the poor—and to other constituencies—when he has some power to share than when he does not. Let me have one more reminiscence and say that I never had more power in relation to the size of the arena than when I was the dean of a faculty at Harvard, and that the effective exercise of that power both permitted and required the maximum feasible participation of the faculty. Nowadays university authorities are faced with a need to share their powers still more widely,

82   but I hazard the guess that the principle may turn out to be the same.

It can be answered that Harvard is a comparatively small place and the power of even the most grasping dean a relatively small matter. This answer is fair. One wayward illustration does not make a proof. To do this sort of thing in government is much harder, and in the government of our cities it sometimes seems impossible. Sometimes the demand for participation conceals a resentment of all authority; sometimes the new participants are too quick to repudiate their own chosen agents; and sometimes the participants, old and new alike, are more concerned with what can be prevented than with what can be accomplished. The conflict between authority and participation may not be logically necessary, but many a harried official has found it inescapable in practice.

It will clearly take us quite a while to learn the theory and practice of a government which reconciles executive authority and popular participation, up and down the line. In the process of learning there will be a heavy premium on patience and durability among our public officials—and a heavy premium also on the kind of leadership, like that of John Kennedy in the nation and John Lindsay in New York, which allows the citizen to participate by a serious identification of his concerns with those of a political leader. (Young radicals who dislike this kind of identification when it occurs within the mainstream of our politics should have a look at their own feelings about the oddly assorted heroes of the New Left.) There is a fine line between democratic leadership and mere personalism, but there is no good case for giving up on the former for fear of the latter.

So it is hard to combine effective government with widespread participation—and harder still while we are learning our way. But we cannot duck the fact that we need both. There is a need for authority; there is a need for participation. The challenge to the philosopher of freedom in our age is not to reject either of these necessities, but to point the way to their creative reconnection in a system of power that is both strong and responsively shared.

In urging the need for a reconstruction of our view of government, I am not merely offering a polite role to the academy. I think it far from plain, indeed, that the academy alone can deal with this problem—it seems too fragmented and too wary, too much devoted to what can be surely demonstrated and too little to what can be done. But I may well be proven wrong. Certainly no one can offer lectures under the auspices of the Kennedy School without a bow to the work of a dozen of its members—and no place is more likely than the university world itself to grow the young men and women who will shed the confining inhibitions of the traditional disciplines to work on the intellectual problem of reconciling authority and freedom in contemporary terms.

And in stating the critical importance of the problem of analysis and exposition I certainly do not intend any offense to those who prefer active participation. There are plenty of issues which are more than ripe for action, and I have the deepest sympathy with those who may feel that the immediate practice of democratic power today is more urgent than its

84   theory. They may be only half right, but fortunately the practitioners too can contribute to the theory; so let us turn to the ways and means of direct action.

*   *   *   *

You choose to be a participant, I am assuming, because you are interested in helping to make things happen. There are many ancillary reasons for seeking a role in government. Fame and glory and meeting interesting people are all parts of it, and the life blood of high politics is and must be intense personal ambition. (One recent book which makes that point clearly and straightforwardly is Randolph Churchill's magnificent life of his father.) But the true object of political ambition is not office alone; it is achievement through office. No life is more painfully empty than that of the man who loves office, electoral or appointive, only for its own sake.

Office-holding is the central form of practical participation in politics—and therefore the center of this part of our discussion. But we must remember that many men affect the action without holding political office. The process of practical politics includes poets and plumbers as well as politicians.

So the test of your participation is not the rank or title you get, but the actual effect of what you do. Here is another argument, incidentally, against arrogance. It does no good to be right if your correct views are so offensively stated that the people whose help you need are put off. What you are interested in is helping the powers of government to work better—not proving your own virtue.

In passing I suggest that this is why you may have to look hard at what is called the politics of protest. I am as far as

can be from suggesting that protest has no place in the politics of participation. To criticize what government does
wrong can be the best way of helping it to do right; the role
of critic is not outside politics, as the careers of Norman
Thomas and Walter Lippmann demonstrate. The question to
be asked about the politics of protest from our present standpoint is simply whether in any particular case the protest
does more good than harm to the cause one is backing. What
does it help to make happen? If it merely makes most of one's
fellow citizens angry, if it gives ammunition to those whose
political objectives are the opposite of yours without advanc-
ing your own cause in any counterbalancing way, or if in
reality it is no more than a somewhat exhibitionist means of
soothing your own conscience, then it is not practical political protest but only what Lenin in another context once called
an infantile disorder. I do not attempt to strike a trial balance
on any particular act of protest; what I do assert is that if you
are serious about the consequences of your actions, you have
to ask and answer these questions.

There is another and closely related question which is
posed by organized protest. In such matters, usually, some
are organizers and some are organized. Group action of this
sort is a complex business, and it can allow some men to use
others without their knowledge or consent. I am not suggesting anything so dull or unreal as that Moscow is managing
these matters in our colleges today. I am saying only that in
my own judgment the right rule for the individual is to be
very sure he knows who is driving before he gets on the bus—
and of course the best way of making sure of that is to help
choose the driver, or even to be the driver yourself. If you

86   mean to have an active and constructive part in the general process of politics as time goes on, it is not good practice to begin by abdicating your responsibility for deciding just what you yourself want to protest, and how. The choice between following your own best judgment and following the leadership of others appears throughout the web of politics. The rules of the game will often impose the acceptance of what others decide; a Presidential assistant, to take a simple case, does not countermand a Presidential order. Moreover, all sustained political effort requires the adjustment of differences in the larger interest, and this must be as true of organized protest as any other form of action. All I am saying is that there are people in the world—including the student world—who like to use other people for their own ends without quite saying what these ends are. One can work with such men in a good cause, but it pays to watch them. I suppose this warning, today, may apply mainly to the very far left; some may find it interesting and even comforting that fifteen years ago it would have applied with equal force— as it may still, for all I know—to the factionalism which then bedeviled the undergraduate Republicans. Just after World War II the place of most serious contest was between a very few Stalinists and the non-Communist liberals; and before World War II . . . but that is another story.

*　*　*　*

To make things happen. Oh, but how? The process of American government is too complex and varied for any man to write a handbook on how to win power. The lack of any

consistent relation between career choice and eventual political significance, in our country, is the despair of analysts,
let alone of young men trying to find their way. It is far from
clear today that the best way to get into public administration
is to study that subject, and it would also be hard to demonstrate that the best way to affect our foreign affairs is to enter
the Foreign Service. Such choices may become more promising if our view of strong government is generally adopted, but
I do not advise anyone to count on it now. When we get to
elective politics, the trouble is even worse. Almost the only
certain rule today is that it helps to be rich, and with any luck
there may be new laws to change that rule before today's
young men are too old to run. And certainly there is no good
way of predicting the chances of those who may hope to move
in and out of the second, third, and fourth levels of the
Executive Branch. This has been my own area of action, and
it was only on the fifth spin of the wheel, in 1961, that I
found myself with a real job to do.

The astonishingly unstructured character of our political
life has two important consequences. The first is that what
passes for career planning among us has to proceed more from
what one *is* than from any estimate of how to get ahead, and
the second is that no matter what you are and what you become, there will probably be opportunities to participate
as time goes on.

Let me pause on this second point before I go back to the
first. I am fearful that in focusing so strongly upon the
Executive Branch of the federal government, and indeed
largely upon the problems of the Presidency itself, I have

88   given a highly distorted image of the range and variety of American politics. I beg you to take seriously the parentheses in which I have noted the highly selective character of my examples and illustrations. In treating the legislative branch so briefly, I have left out a host of important activities and opportunities. There are many kinds of Congressmen and Senators; they and the members of their staffs have a large role in government now and are likely to have a larger one in the future. What is still more serious is that I have said almost nothing about state and local government. Even if the money for great undertakings comes more and more from the federal treasury—as I think it must—the real process of action on much of what most needs doing will be in state capitals and in the cities.

A most striking example of local need and opportunity is public education. I have already remarked that public school systems are a major part of our system of government. Most of them are very badly run. Especially in our larger cities they have become enmeshed in a tangle of negative powers which makes them extraordinarily resistant to change, and they are currently failing to do the job that this new age demands of them. They do not have the money, the public support, the leadership, the teachers, the buildings, the atmosphere, the energy, or the concept of their meaning that they need. This is partly a problem for the Schools of Education, but it is also a problem and an opportunity for those who mean to participate in government. There is no field of action in this country which offers larger opportunity for first-rate men. It is not an accident that the two Commis-

sioners of Education who have held office in these last years,
as the necessary revolution slowly begins, Francis Keppel
and Harold Howe, are two of the very few first-rate men of
their generation who chose to make public education their
profession. I don't suppose either of them set out to hold
that particular office. They set out from where they were and
what they cared about—which was the quality of education
in the context of the needs of society. During the next
twenty years the country will need thousands of leaders in
public education to carry forward what a mere handful have
started. That leadership, profoundly political in one sense,
will also have to be profoundly professional in another. It
will have to be the spearhead of a revolution which trans-
forms our public school world from a political system marked
by impotence and irresponsibility into one marked by authority, accountability, and much wider community participation.

And that takes me back to my first point: that you have to
begin from what you are, not from the office you want to
hold. In that sense the conscious decision to be a participant does not decide much. In the nuclear problem, for
example, one can participate as a scientist, as an economist,
as a publicist, as a lawyer, as a military man, or as a professional politician. In communications the range of needed
skills is just as wide, and in the war against racism and poverty
it is even wider.

What I am suggesting is that in addition to the decision to
participate—with all its presumption and all its implications
of commitment and sympathy—a young man must choose
to become someone with something to offer. Fifty years ago

90 Alfred North Whitehead made his majestic pronouncement that "In the conditions of modern life the rule is absolute; the race which does not value trained intelligence is doomed." For this generation and for its members as participants that rule is personal; if you do not train yourself to something, you are doomed to the role of dilettante. I do not mean at all that you must stay in school forever mastering a particular learned discipline. That is one way, but certainly not the only way, to give oneself a role.

But which skill to seek? I cannot answer that question. Where there is a clear bent, it usually makes sense to follow it. I would add that if there is a serious family tradition you should think twice before you turn away from it. There is a curious and interesting tendency of later generations to be more public-minded than earlier ones; and to succeed to an established role can save extremely valuable time. Obviously this rule does not apply when there is strong distaste for the tribal trade, and moreover there is more than one way to build on a family position, as the lives of Averell Harriman and John F. Kennedy suggest. Still I respect the reinforcement of tradition, and names like Adams and Roosevelt remind us that this is not an un-American notion.

But what if neither personal bent nor family tradition is decisive? No question is more often asked of those who are supposed to know about these things, and none is harder to answer. If the arts and the ministry clearly require a vocation, other activities are less demanding; and I repeat that even those who feel no call should have a trade.

The most traditional choice of the undecided has been the
law. It is an honorable and varied profession; it can be both
a good thing to do and a good way of deferring a decision.
Moreover, lawyers tend to live well enough—if seldom sump-
tuously—and they have a profession that allows them to go
back and forth to government somewhat more readily than
most. But behind these tactical reasons for the choice of the
law there is a deeper and better argument that has to do with
the practical reconciliation of the varied ends and means of
decent government. If we are to build the laws and the
institutions that are needed for the kind of stronger government I have been urging, lawyers must be among the principal
architects and carpenters. The most immediate example of
the opportunities of the lawyer today may be in the reform
of his own profession, from the courts to the classroom, but
the lawyer will always have a large role on the wider stage of
government. At the membranes between all institutions and
all forms of government we find the lawyer.

But lawyers do not have a monopoly on relevance, as the
best of them are quick to recognize. Consider science, for
example. The scientist as scientist can be a powerful political
force—will any politician do more for political economy in
this century than the men and women who really solve the
technology of birth control? And the scientist (both pure and
applied) as political participant is a good and major force that
must grow. Economics? Possibly a more constraining choice,
but also a very good one if you want a scarce and highly
valued license to join nearly any team. The other social

92   sciences?   Chancier, but full of high intellectual interest
in their own right, and perhaps nearer the intellectual fron-
tier of the process of government than they were a generation
ago, or than much of economics is now. Management (business or other)? A very promising possibility, both for its own
importance in society and because it is a calling which is
likely to have much more relation to government in your
generation than it seemed to have in mine. Robert McNamara
is certainly not the last graduate of a business school to make
a contribution to the management of government—nor is
George Romney the last of business leaders to turn to the
polls.

Somewhere beyond these traditional callings there may be
a more general classification that may be still more significant for the next generation of those who take part in government: this is the class of those who can reduce great qualita-
tive issues to practical questions of choice in the use of
resources. The men who can do this sort of thing go by many
names: not only economists and managers, but program
planners, systems analysts, masters of operations research,
and sometimes, grandly, decision makers. What they all
have in common, when they do these things well, is a respect
for the relation between what goes in and what comes out.
Their way of thinking does not exhaust the process of government, nor does it define the answers to the hardest social and
political questions, but neither can these questions be
answered if this way of thought is neglected. Its power is
essential to our hope of making the technology of the future
our servant and not our master.

It is a foolish know-nothing error to suppose that this kind of skill is the necessary enemy of freedom. The truth is the opposite: those who want to make a complex society work for freedom will have to master the trades by which one can understand how the choices a society makes can produce the results it wants. Not to learn to use these new skills for freedom is senseless reaction.

Let me turn now from this new world of science to a world which will always have much room for art—the world of journalism. It is a strange trade, with lots of room at the bottom and much less at the top, and we have James Reston himself to tell us that it is not as important as it thinks it is.* Moreover, I think it can be a mistake to suppose that because one likes working on a college paper the next step is professional journalism; the college paper is often a form of intense political participation, and journalism in the wide world is much more an observer's game. Mr. Reston thinks it is less participatory than it should be (although he is thinking more of reporters and editors than publishers), and I agree with him. Indeed the insistence on apartness which characterizes some self-righteous newspapers seems foolish. It seems close to a scandal, for example, that *The New York Times* should have refused to take part in a study of the relation between riots and reporting which was conducted by the President's Commission on Civil Disorders on the ground that the subject was an improper one for the commission to consider. (It may be still more remarkable that *The Times* did not report its own refusal.)

* Cf. James B. Reston, *The Artillery of the Press,* Harper & Row, 1967.

94   Journalism in its wider sense—as the main instrument of
our intercommunication and the main critic of our political
performance—the journalism that embraces television,
books and magazines, as well as the daily press—this
journalism deserves recruits, in the next generation, from the
very top rank of those who mean to have a part. In a sense,
indeed, the politician himself, and even the appointed official, must understand this wider art of communication, not
only from expert to expert, but out to the viewing and the
reading public. If we are to have more effective government,
one element of it will be better communication about government, at all levels. Moreover, the revolution in communications which I have touched on as an example of the need for
government is itself a challenge to the coming generation.
Who will get to use the new skills of this new journalism?
The distance from "The Front Page" to the best present-day
journalism is very great, and yet we are only at the beginning.

                        *   *   *   *

So there are many attractive trades for those who mean
to take part in government. Every skill has its own requirements and offers its own delights, and they all charge the
same high price for mastery: the price is effort. The one to
choose is the one that feels right, and I think most men can
have two tries in their twenties.

The paradox of time when you are young is that you have
both more and less of it than you want. If I am not mistaken,
much of the protest in the student world today derives from

impatience at exclusion from power and not simply from the feeling that those in power are doing things wrong. I cannot give much direct comfort here—it is very hard indeed for individuals to affect events when they are young. Only the most gifted or the most happily placed can hope to do that on any large scale in their twenties or even their early thirties. The individual young man can certainly make trouble (which is not always a bad thing), and as he finds particular chances he can do particular kinds of good that can be very important where they happen. Moreover young people in large numbers can have the same effect that other large groups have had, throughout our history, when deeply stirred; this is the lesson of the primaries of 1968. But to have a positive *personal* effect on the process of national government is much harder, and in nearly all cases it takes longer.

So when you are young you have time; but you need it, and for four reasons. The first, as I have said, is that you need a skill—you need to have a trained intelligence, and it should be trained for something. Precisely because government is chancy and changing, moreover, the man who intends to have a direct role in it needs such a skill so that he can keep his own freedom of movement. If you are really good at something, there is always somewhere else to go.

The second need for time is the complement of the first. As a man learns the trade he chooses, he needs also to learn to understand what other men are like and how they think. This is the point I was struggling with earlier as I tried to tell how failure of understanding has hampered the government

96   in the nuclear field. If you mean to bear a hand in government—at whatever level—you will need not only your own skill and concern, but understanding of the skills and concerns of others, and especially of those you may oppose. Fortunately, the mastery of one craft is a first step, if you will use it, to the understanding of another, just as the learning of a first foreign language makes the next one easier. That there is no necessity about this is apparent from the troubles that very able men have had, in our recent history, in understanding other skills and other problems than their own. Here the most remarkable current illustration may be the case of George Kennan, one of the best men of our age. His brilliant autobiography demonstrates that he combined a truly remarkable diplomatic intelligence with an almost complete intolerance of the process of politics within his own government. He also accomplished the astonishing feat of combining intense humanity with uncompromising elitism. His kind of talent is sorely needed in government, but our process will always tend to reject the elitist, unless (like Admiral Rickover, for example) he takes out the sort of political insurance a Kennan would scorn.

What I hope for from you is a general sympathy with the variety of the skills and perspectives which are essential to government, and I think the university can be a good place to be getting it. The university does not contain every kind of man and woman—it is short of farmers, workers, soldiers, and even real live politicians. But it has a lot of variety in it. You can learn here not only "the habitual vision of greatness" (the phrase again is Whitehead's), but also, if you will, the habit of sympathetic respect for variety.

Let me underline the point by one more reference to the nuclear problem. I see here both a special hazard and a special opportunity for your generation. Youth is at once a time of necessary specialization and a time when sympathy can be stirred for the special concerns of others. You and your contemporaries, whether scientists, cadets, or would-be politicians, are well placed to get it clearly in mind that the great and dangerous choices of the nuclear age can be made wisely, down through the years, only if those who share in making the decisions can draw not only on specialists but on specialists who have learned to understand one another. The nuclear problem is the instance *par excellence* of the pervasive need for interconnection among experts, and I shall be both surprised and disappointed if the coming generation cannot do that job better than it has been done so far.

The third reason you need time is that you have a lot to do. If you aim high, as you should, then the sooner you put the mark of your own excellence on something, the better. You may not greatly affect events in your twenties, but it is good to establish your identity in those years, not only to yourself but as a member of your society. To be noticed is not necessarily to be famous, or to have your name in the papers. It is simply to make a mark where other men with your concern can see it and come to expect much of you. That can happen in a hundred ways; the one thing it nearly always demands is work, and its principal advantage is that when you have once learned to compete in this honorable way, you are likely to go on.

98   I am far from believing, however, that work is all the twenties are for, or that all is lost if no clear mark is made in that
decade.   Youth is a time for lightness of heart and even irresponsibility as well as a time for intense effort and some
presumption.   There is far more to life than is dreamed of in
the particular philosophy I am preaching here, and I doubt
if men and women can make themselves fit to help govern for
freedom if they do not also learn a little of what freedom itself
is for and how to use it.   These things too take time—they are
the fourth reason you need it.

The politics of our age demand men who are somehow
whole, men who have gone beyond learning alone, beyond
the cheerful sampling of life's various joys, even beyond the
confident establishment of identity.

The whole man—the man who sees life itself as the gift
and his use of it as the test—is not found only in the field of
politics. John Kennedy used to quote the Greeks to the effect
that the challenge of existence is to use all one's powers along
lines of excellence, but nothing in that definition prescribes
politics as the necessary center of concern.   In my own
generation, on that test, I would not want to set any politician
—except perhaps Kennedy himself—against the poet Lowell
or the inventor Land or the physicist Purcell or the novelist
Styron. Indeed I am willing to draw a long bow and say that
the political man who is only that is somehow unfit for the
decades we now face. It seems to me likely that such a man
will have a dangerous absence of self-knowledge—that in
making modern politics and its ambitions the whole of his
life he may run the risk of never knowing who he is and
what he believes in. Such a man is unfit for politics.

I have urged the need for experts, but I would hope you might become the kind of expert who respects not only the value of other men's skill, but the relevance of your own life as a man. In such a broader concept of what you are, there is protection against a danger which is created by the very expertise which I have praised. I have been warning against the kind of specialized skill which does not try to understand and respect the professional skills of others. It is fitting to warn still more briskly against the kind of expertise which becomes a substitute for manhood. Precisely because the world is crowded, complex, and full of pressure for conformity, it is the simple human duty of all of us not only to respect the individuality of others, but also to cultivate our own. We need boldness in living our own lives, and generosity toward the like decisions of others. This requires more than respect for skill or position. No man is adequately described by calling him a physicist, or an official, or a Senator; he is also a man. So are you, and the kind of man you turn out to be will depend heavily on what you ask of yourself between the ages of fifteen and thirty. If you ask little, then indeed you may find yourself at thirty no more than an organism with a trade. It is not a good result, not even for your part in politics.

A man's nature, his sense of what he is and means, necessarily precedes his political role, if any—both in time and in meaning. And the point is just as sharp the other way around: a man's politics, for their own sake, require that he know who he is. Take the question of the Negro in America. Here is a case where everything you can do as a participant in government will depend heavily on what you think—indeed on what

100   you are—as a man. This is another way of saying that the
problem of the American Negro is first and foremost a
problem in the American mind. On this subject the American
mind as a whole—both white and black—is a shambles.
Yours, if you mean to be a useful participant, will have to be
clearer, more fully stocked, harder, more sensitive, and somehow set free from prejudice, hate, and guilt. This is not a
small task.

The partisans of liberal education are not wrong, therefore,
when they tell you that one great element in your preparation
for the world of action must be an exposure to some part—
a part because you cannot examine it all—of the kaleido-
scope of behavior and misbehavior—of art and fraud—
of gold and tinsel—which is our inheritance. The humanities
have their absolute values, of course, but I speak here of their
value for politics. History is a powerful solvent of prejudice; literature is a warning against vanity; and to test yourself as a human being in such studies is to have a chance of
learning both the possibility and the difficulty of real performance in the real world. The liberal curriculum is right,
in short, when it attempts to give equal honor to what one
must learn because one is a man and what one must learn
because a subject is a subject. All that I would add is that
this double requirement does not end—indeed it intensifies
—after graduation.

*   *   *   *

But if you mean to be a participant, there are two
special things you should get into your youth if you can.

They are the two greatest elements of politics, so that if you
have any gift for them you should find it out. Even if your own
contribution must be made in other ways, the more you
understand of these two the better. They are the analysis
of political ideas and the practice of elective politics—the
real ends and means against which all the rest is merely
instrumental.

I have already asked for your help in building a new theory
of effective government. This is part, but only part, of the
intellectual agenda of politics. We certainly need government, but we also need to be clear about the things that
government should be doing—about the political agenda
of our time.

The ends of our political life, the issues of each next
stage, are formulated by a process of national thought in
which all sorts of men and women take part. Only occa-
sionally in this process does the defining idea emerge from
the government itself. The agenda of today is framed not
only by explosive events but by the reaction of reasoning
men to these events. In this process we pass beyond the
functional or instrumental role of the economist, the lawyer,
the scientist, and the rest, and we move into the area where
the democratic process originates: the generation of a political
idea. This is seldom a wholly individual process; our society
is pluralistic in its political imagination. Yet there can be no
denial that these ideas come from human minds—reform of
education, reconstruction of welfare, flexible taxes, remaking
of public policy on communications, and new proposals for
nuclear safety—all these must depend upon the disciplined

102 and directed imagination of men. And so, still more, does the general case for stronger government which I have been sketching.

There is no one calling which can fit a man for a part in this process—no discipline and no institution has a monopoly on the good political idea. I believe that here again it is hard to play without a trained intelligence, but first-class political ideas have found their first voice among Americans in all kinds of places. It happens, I think, that in the last generation or so there has been no single outstanding political thinker; we have done better with bits and pieces of invention than with the imaginative reframing of our political thought. Perhaps that is because in part our basic political thought is really all right—perhaps my very first premise is right and we really do know what we mean by freedom. As I have said, you will want to ask if that is so, but I hope you will also go on and put your own mind to work out at the edges where purpose and practice meet. It is not at all too soon for young men to bear a hand in framing the political agenda of the future. In that sense even ineffective protest can have future meaning. You may well find that you graduate into the small company of men who continue through their lives in this creative role. The country has too few of them, and no single group has greater weight in shaping our society.

The other field to explore is active politics, and here I speak not of administration or management, critically needed as they are, but of the embattled activity of winning elections and passing laws. It is good to see this battle from as close as you can, either as a direct participant or as the committed supporter of a participant. To watch it as an observer, even very close in, is not the same thing. Neither the political scientist nor the political reporter can tell you what the front lines of the democratic process really feel like; you have to be there yourself. The practicing politician deserves respect for what he faces, for the power he wins to act, and for his pre-eminent role in representing the people to the government and the government to the people.

* * * *

I have been assuming that participation is what you want. Perhaps as I come toward the end I ought to recognize again that this is a lot to assume. My reasons for the assumption were practical and not moral—first, it has been my own assumption, and a man argues best from his own premises; second, problems like the three I have chosen as practical examples simply cannot be dealt with except through government; third, I think that when a reasonable man considers the chances of revolution against those of reform, in this country, he must conclude that to choose revolution is to choose futility and even counterproductivity. I object to left-wing revolutionary sentiment on a lot of other grounds, but its combination of functional irrelevance and political counterproductivity are enough for now, without resort to questions of liberty, decency, and observed performance elsewhere. I recognize and praise in the American radical left a healthy capacity to see a part of what is wrong, but I find in it no promise of an ability to put things right, which is

104   the most interesting part of the problem. I would make an equal rejection of the so-called politics of the radical right. It is stronger among our people, of course, and always has been, but it lacks a rational program, and it would come apart in civil war if it ever tried to design one. The far left and the far right—even if one of them fills Madison Square Garden and the other a governor's chair or two—are outside the range of the politics I believe in.

Beyond that I do not choose up sides. If pressed, I would say that on national performance in the last thirty-five years, the attitude I am urging has found more friends among Democrats than among Republicans, among liberals than among conservatives, among Northerners than among Southerners, and among professors than among "practical" people. But I will add at once that if you mean to talk about truly effective government, even in Democratic Administrations, you will find yourself talking about a lot of men who are independents and Republicans, and the sort of executive energy I have praised—an energy which extends from programs to performance—has been found as much among progressive Republican governors, in the last twenty years, as anywhere else. If you answer that at the national level what starts and stops these programs is the Congress, then I would have to praise the liberal Democrats and a handful of progressive Republicans. But I would answer once again that those who enact a program and those who make it work are not identical.

So I resist partisan conclusions. They are misleading as often as not, and they are especially misleading if they persuade us that the real decision on any great change in our national attitudes will come from within a political party alone. That is not the way our political life works. If we are to have stronger and more accountable government in the next twenty years, we will have it not because liberal Democrats or progressive Republicans want it, but because the country wants it. That is the point some of my friends among academic liberals tend to forget, and that our common leader President Kennedy always remembered. The intellectual task before any reformer is not to persuade his own happy few, but to persuade the country.

Here we have one more reason for a decent respect to the American mind as a whole, and a continuing sympathy with all our fellow citizens, not just with those who think as we do. The politics of consensus is not a new invention, but a historical necessity, and more than that it is good for us. It is another reminder that whatever our skills and our insights, we are members of a larger society which retains the right of final choice. If we are to have adequate government for freedom in our time, the American people will have to decide that they want it. It is a fair challenge to us all.

This last point about political ideas and political action reinforces still further my hope that you may test them both. Both issues and elective battles, when they have real meaning (and of course not all of them do), bring us face to face with the fundamental mystery of our political life—our faith in the eventual opinions of America. One of the half-submerged premises of our political life, and of this book, is that when the issues and the men are sorted out, when the champions

106   of what is right are as lively as those of what is no longer
right, we can count on our people to make choices that work
for freedom. We have no time to take that mystery to pieces,
even if we knew how, but before we stop we must take a
moment to consider it.

What it means, quite simply, is that the final custodians
of the American idea are the American people—not the experts, not the creative thinkers, not even the politicians
certified by combat. I may persuade you that we need
stronger government, but until the nation is persuaded,
my notion will be unreal. To make things happen they must
be made to happen in the American mind, and no man alone
makes up this country's mind—our people do that for
themselves. I am aware of the skills that have been shown
in our history, by good men and bad, in the art of persuasion.
That art has enormous importance, and I urge it as one of the
best reasons for asserting yourself both in political ideas and
political contests. In politics as elsewhere all that is needed
for bad men to triumph is for good men to do nothing; and
the power of the art of persuasion in the age of mass communication is a massive reinforcement of that old rule. What
I am also saying, however, is that the greatest of all our
politicians had it right when he said that you can't fool all
of the people all of the time. If you mean to take part in
politics, and really serve freedom, you must know the public
as yourself and respect not only its right, but its capacity,
to decide.

And now, because I am addressing a university audience,
I will offer one last thought. We have talked about the theory

of democratic action, about the necessary qualities of the participant, about the honor of political combat, and about the mystery of faith in democracy. Surely the idea of the university is with us as we talk of such things. The university values man and his reason, not only for their own sake but for their part in the good life of society. You do not desert this standard when you presume to participate, or when you seek to persuade your countrymen to back your program, or even to back you. The university is no friend to inactivity or resignation, no partner in the repudiation of the American hope. From our colleges and universities Americans have gone out for three centuries to join their lives with their country's life in building a free society. If what is needed now is stronger government for freedom, must one not expect and even demand that the university man of this generation should enlist?

Index